MORE TALES FROM THE MESS

By the same author

Tales From the Mess

MORE TALES
FROM THE MESS
Miles Noonan

CENTURY PUBLISHING
LONDON

Copyright © Miles Noonan 1985
All rights reserved
First published in Great Britain in 1985
by Century Publishing Co. Ltd,
Portland House,
12–13 Greek Street, London W1V 5LE
Set in Linoterm Baskerville by The Castlefield Press,
Moulton, Northampton
Printed and bound in Great Britain by
Anchor Brendon Ltd, Tiptree, Essex

British Cataloguing in Publication Data
Noonan, Miles
    More tales from the mess.
    1. Great Britain, Army——Anecdotes, facetiae, satire, etc.
    I. Title
    355'.00941   ——UA649
    ISBN 0 7126 1067 7

The author and publishers thank the proprietors
for permission to include *Punch* cartoons
in *More Tales from the Mess*.

CONTENTS

FOREWORD

The nucleus of the panel of reminiscing old-timers, suppliers of much of the material for the first instalment of *Tales From the Mess*, is still in being and has been enlarged. It has attracted to itself fresh contributors of comparable reliability.

The caveat that it was necessary to attach to the earlier collection carries similar force with the second. The qualification for an entry's inclusion has stayed unchanged. If something has been *said* to have happened it has gone in, without any nonsense about the mounting of fussy researches to confirm its authenticity.

This cautious disclaimer should not be interpreted as a reflection upon either the integrity or the sincerity of my collaborators. I am deeply grateful to them, and hold them entirely responsible for any inaccuracies that might have crept into this book.

Miles Noonan

QUIS CUSTODIET?

I N the nineteenth century, when tigers had not yet become an endangered species and were still a great threat in rural India to livestock and, to a lesser but still lethal extent, to humans, tiger shooting was a respectable sport. It required skill, courage, patience and quick-wittedness. It could be dangerous. It could yield lasting evidence of success. After taxidermy, large enduring trophies were available for display about the house, ultimately to decorate or to disfigure, according to spectator reaction, the homes of retired *pukkha sahibs* in places like Cheltenham and Budleigh Salterton in which the reminiscences of old men about how they shot the hearthrug generated in their grandchildren either admiration or revulsion.

Two officers of the 5th Lancers, on leave in the Terai, shot a tigress during the hot weather of 1869. In its death spasms it sprang and fastened on to the arm of one of its killers. His arm had to be amputated and he died in hospital two days later. At the site of the shooting there were found to be deep, instinctive reasons, beyond anger at being attacked, for the tigress's ferocity. She had had two young cubs with her.

The injured big game hunter, the body of the tiger and the cubs were carried back to base by the beaters. The cubs were taken to Lucknow. There, one cub died. The other was presented to the Royal Madras Fusiliers, for whom it became the regimental mascot. It was named Plassey, after the regiment's most memorable battle in which the force commander had been a former Madras Fusilier officer, Robert Clive.

The origins of the Madras Fusiliers dated back to the days of the Honourable East India Company. 'John Company' was a huge commercial enterprise with its headquarters in the city of London and with quasi-governmental auspices; it underpinned its trading activities by providing both the civil administration of that part of India in which it operated (which was most of it) and the armed forces needed to support the administration. The majority of John Company's troops, who at their peak numbered more than 200,000 was Indian. A tiny minority of regiments were exclusively European. The Madras Fusiliers was one of these.

After the Indian Mutiny of 1857, largely engaged in by units of the company's Bengal army, John Company was dissolved and India became the direct responsibility of the Crown. The Company's European regiments were incorporated *en bloc* into the Queen's army, a not entirely popular measure that stimulated one of the earliest recorded sit-down strikes in either military or industrial history. The British army paid less, took discipline more seriously and had different terms of service. To turn volunteers for one army into conscripts for another, without consulting them, was to ask for trouble.

The discontent was mollified by the customary mixture of coercion, conciliation and bluff. Little of this remained an issue by the time that Plassey put in his appearance as the regimental mascot, but one ramification was of relevance. The Fusiliers, in their 250-odd years of existence, had been stationed outside India only twice, for brief periods in both Burma and in the Dutch East Indies, and they were now liable for home service. They were posted to Dover. They brought with them both Plassey and an inherited collective attitude to the small change of day-to-day life better suited to India than to the United Kingdom.

Plassey was by then almost fully grown. From the time of his adoption he had been put in the care of a soldier with a natural love for, and understanding of animals. Plassey was well brought up. He was gentle, biddable and affectionate. In India he had been led by his keeper around barracks and bazaars on a leading rein. Passing soldiers greeted him with friendly pats on the back, tickles behind the ears and strokings of his coat. He and his keeper marched in front of the band on ceremonial parades, and he was brought around the table to be petted at guest nights in the officers' mess. He had been accepted into regimental society in the same manner and spirit as would have been a big, cheerful dog of unusual configuration. It occurred to nobody that what seemed normal in Lucknow might look different in a small coastal town in Kent.

The shopkeepers were the first to complain. They could think of few more powerful ways of discouraging shoppers, they said, than for them to be suddenly confronted by a large Bengal tiger padding down the High Street on a dog lead held by an unarmed soldier. The shopkeepers sent a delegation to Colonel Raikes to discuss their reservations. They didn't make much progress. Plassey, the colonel explained patiently, might look alarming to the uninitiated, but he was as peaceful as a lamb. He was in the control of a responsible, reliable and experienced handler. The people of Dover would soon get used to Plassey, an affable and unaggressive tiger who wouldn't harm a fly.

The shopkeepers left, unconvinced and defeated. Plassey continued to be taken on his daily walk around the town. An increasing number of the residents of Dover took to shopping in Folkestone. As trade fell off, and nervous collapses burgeoned, opposition to Plassey strengthened. Action was demanded of the mayor. His interview with Colonel Raikes was as sterile as that with the shopkeepers had been. The colonel was courteous but adamant: Plassey was harmless and had always been harmless. All that the citizens of Dover had to do was to show a little adaptability.

The colonel did, however, make one concession towards municipal opinion. If Plassey, against all precedent, showed the least sign of becoming a danger to human life then Plassey would go. The mayor left, wondering bitterly what the colonel's definition of a threat to human life was.

Plassey threatened human life a few days later. He had been fed, bedded in his cage and stroked to sleep by his keeper. The keeper then went out on the town and got riotously drunk. An attempt by the sergeant of the guard to confine him when he returned noisily to the gate led to a scuffle, the disengagement of the keeper and a chase within barracks led by the sergeant and with two of the guard in tow. It all seemed pretty pointless to the sergeant. The keeper was simply adding to the charges against himself by trying to evade capture in a walled enclosure from which the only way out was one gate. Beside the gate was the guardroom.

Much the same line of thought passed through the mind of the keeper, until he had an idea. He sprinted for Plassey's cage, jumped in, lay down beside Plassey and immediately fell asleep. Plassey awoke briefly, and put a protective foreleg on his friend's shoulder. Then Plassey went back to sleep too. It was when the pursuit party reached the cage that Plassey lost his temper.

The sergeant, who was as well-disposed towards Plassey as was everyone else in the battalion, had never seen him like this before. Plassey made it snarlingly clear, with an extensive exposure of claw to reinforce the message, that any attempt to disturb the rest of his friend the keeper would provoke instant mayhem.

The sergeant withdrew. The keeper had a good night's sleep. So did Plassey.

On the following morning the keeper fondled Plassey and then, rather sheepishly, gave himself up.

On the day after that the keeper was sentenced to twenty-eight days' detention, Plassey was donated to the Zoological Gardens, and the mayor, shopkeepers and citizens of Dover cheered up for the first time in weeks.

Plassey lived on in the zoo for seven years. When he died his head was mounted and was presented to the officers' mess. There had by then been another of the army's periodical reorganizations, and the Madras Fusiliers had amalgamated with another regiment to form the 1st Battalion of the Royal Dublin Fusiliers. Plassey's head looked down from various walls upon the revels, joys and sorrows of this itinerant home, in which as a young, live tiger Plassey had been welcomed on guest nights, until the regiment was disbanded after the setting up of the Irish Free State in 1922.

Nobody seems to know what happened to Plassey's mounted head after that.

YOU MUST BE KIDDING

BEFORE the war with the Boer Republics of the Transvaal and the Orange Free State started in 1899, there was a period of indecision and dissension in British politico-military circles about the size and nature of the reinforcements needed to bring up to a suitable strength the garrisons of the British parts of South Africa, Natal and Cape Colony.

Whatever composition would be finally settled upon, it was clear that extra artillery would be required. Some of this was sent in 1898. From it, twenty field guns, with their normal accompanying organization of officers, NOCs, gunners, limbers, horses, transport and the rest, went to the major British base of Ladysmith, in northern Natal.

Some days after they had settled in, a demonstration shoot was arranged, with these new, up-to-date guns. Among the guests was a group of local Boer farmers, included on the invitation list less from an urge to show hospitality than a calculated determination to apply psychological pressure. The farmers, it was rightly thought, would waste no time before spreading word across the border to their fellow-Boers of the effectiveness of modern artillery, professionally manned and controlled.

A low ridge named Wagon Hill was chosen as the target area. Twenty live goats were tethered to stakes on the hill. At a range of three thousand yards, the twenty guns fired shrapnel for twenty minutes at the goats.

THE INTELLIGENCE DEPARTMENT

First Budding General. 'I SAY, IS THAT JOHNNIE ON THE HILL A SCOUT OR A WRETCHED CIVILIAN?'
Second Budding Gereral: 'MY DEAR CHAP, *DO* YOU TAKE ME FOR A SORT OF SHERLOCK HOLMES?'

At the end of this bombardment the spectators were led to the hill to inspect the casualties. There were now twenty-two live goats: the original twenty, none of which had been hit, and two kids, born during the shelling.

THE GORDON HUMP

ONE of the signs that distinguishes a good general, so good generals, bad generals, and military historians let it be known, is preparedness to refuse to do things that other influential people think that it would be a good thing to do. The good general, pressed for political, or propaganda, or in some cases purely idiotic, reasons to take a course of action that he knows to be militarily unsound, digs his heels in and points forcibly to the disadvantages of such a course of action.

Thus, during the Second World War, General Sir Alan Brooke, the Chief of the Imperial General Staff, spent much of his time – usually in the middle of the night when he wanted to go to bed and Mr Winston Churchill didn't – in the production and development of persuasive arguments about the unwisdom of pursuing such schemes of Mr Churchill's as the establishment of an unsupported beach-head beyond the range of fighter cover in Norway, or tying up and probably losing most of the commandos in the purposeless capture of the island of Pantellaria or doing something aggressively spectacular but fundamentally useless in the north of Sumatra. (These and a great many other aberrations aside, General Brooke had an enormous admiration for Mr Churchill as a war leader.)

In the simpler days of Victorian soldiering, the reasons that were put forward for doing or not doing things were of a less complex politico-strategic nature than the ones that Brooke had to dream up in the small hours of the morning at No. 10 Downing Street or at Chequers.

A case in point arose during a planning conference chaired by General Sir Garnet Wolseley in 1884 to discuss arrangements for the relief of General Charles Gordon, at the time besieged in Khartoum by Dervishes under the leadership of the Mahdi.

It was believed by some, not least among them Mr Gladstone the Liberal Prime Minister, that Gordon's incarceration at Khartoum was a product of his own high-minded obstinacy.

Gordon was a remarkable sapper of deep religious faith, an unfashionable tendency to pass his spare time in the performance of good works among the poor and the sick, and, for a Victorian, an almost subversive indifference to money, which he mainly either gave away when he had it, or refused to accept when it was offered to him. He was an outstandingly able soldier with a particular flair for getting the best out of those who in his time were comprehensively known as 'natives'.

He had been famously successful as the commander of the Chinese Ever Victorious Army during the Taiping Rebellion against the Imperial Chinese government, and caused distress and amazement to the Chinese court by resigning when one of their acts met with his moral disapproval. He upset them further by sending back the handsome financial present with which they wanted to reward him for his services. He had governed the Equatorial Province of Central Africa. He had been sent to the Sudan to superintend the evacuation of the Egyptian administration and garrison, neither of which was humane, efficient or a match for the Mahdi and his Fuzzie-Wuzzies. Gordon had got some out, but refused to obey an order to abandon the ones that he couldn't get out and to get out by himself.

The unhappy Egyptian warriors, not celebrated for their martial ardour, congregated around General Gordon in Khartoum. He inspired them to fight for their lives, and with a compound of ingenuity, leadership, and zeal had by the time of Wolseley's planning conference already survived a siege of

17

five months.*

The delay over even starting to think about how to rescue Gordon was of almost entirely political provenance. Mr Gladstone mistrusted imperial adventures, and had good reason to suspect the army of fostering them. He feared that if an insufficiently strong force were to be sent to aid Gordon it could meet with the same fate as Hicks Pasha and his Egyptians had earlier suffered at the hands of the formidable Fuzzie-Wuzzies – total obliteration. Should that happen, public outrage would ensure that Britain would become embroiled in a major and expensive campaign in an intrinsically valueless expanse of desert for no reasons other than revenge and the restoration of national prestige.

Mr Gladstone temporized until public opinion, and the imminence of a general election, forced him to decide. The timing of his authorization of an expedition was a rare example of how to squeeze the last drop of the worst out of everything: an expensive enterprise mounted too late to achieve its objective – the recovery of a disobeyer of orders – that led to a failure which had to be redeemed by an even more expensive retributive, and successful, expedition commanded by Lord Kitchener thirteen years later.

The planners at the Wolseley conference were exclusively from the Wolseley ring, enterprising and ambitious officers who had followed the Wolseley star through a series of campaigns from the Red River in Canada to a previous devastatingly successful venture in Egypt, by way of the Gold Coast and various parts of Southern Africa. They were all practical men, innovators, reformers, committed to demonstrating that merit, and not birth and wealth, should determine professional military advancement.

They had each studied the problem of how to get a force of seven thousand men over a distance of twelve hundred miles along a route that for reasons of water supply would have to follow the Nile. Aside from watering the soldiers and animals,

---

* All told, he was to hold out for nine months. Gordon was killed, and the defences of Khartoum were overrun, six days before Wolseley's relief column arrived within range of the city.

the Nile offered a highway upon which boats could transport provisions of all sorts. But there were disadvantages. The Nile wound its way in erratic loops, and its smooth surface between Cairo and Khartoum was broken by six cataracts, around which all stores, and such boats as were needed for further progress up river, would have to be manhandled.

It was agreed by those with experience of them on the Red River that the best boatmen to deal with the vagaries of the Nile, and with the portages at the cataracts, would be Canadian *voyageurs*.

A suitable mounted force, capable of speeding matters up by cutting across the necks of the river's loops, would clearly be required. Horses would not survive the desert. A Camel Corps of mounted infantry was needed. Arrangements were put in hand to requisition a selected number of camels and for them to be assembled, along with a huge conglomeration of other supplies, at Korti, three hundred miles upstream from Cairo, and the best available jumping-off point. It was accepted that despite the biological adaptability of camels to desert conditions, large numbers of them would die during the extremes of endurance to which they would have to be put.

The conference went quietly and efficiently on, the sequence logical, the proceedings orderly, the suggestions constructive.

One prominent member of the Wolseley Ring said nothing at all. Little surprise was caused by this taciturnity. General Sir Redvers Buller was renowned as a man of deeds rather than of words. He was in many ways the archetype of a Victorian soldierly hero, and in many others the antithesis of Gordon. Whereas Gordon was a charismatic philanthropist with an elaborately stocked mind and an inspired delicacy of touch, Buller went in for what generations later would be known as bashing on regardless. He was fearless and of powerful physique. He was a VC. He had intermittently had large and important bits of himself shot away and had given no indication that he noticed their absence. These surgical setbacks had been complemented by an extraordinary proneness to infection by exotic diseases, which he overcame with the same determined contempt that he applied to the effects of his wounds.

By origin Buller was a Devon squire. He was solicitous about the well-being of his tenants and of his livestock, just as he was loved by his troops for the care that he took to make sure that they were as comfortably accommodated and properly fed as circumstances would permit. He was less benevolent with his officers, and with those of equal or superior rank with whom he had to work. Buller's judgements on their performances were reached arbitrarily and expressed tersely. A litter of wrecked commissioned psyches mingled with the evidence of physical mayhem that he left behind him in the arenas of his innumerable small campaigns.

When most of the outlines of the Khartoum plan had been agreed, Wolseley asked Buller if he had anything to contribute. Buller had. He said that it was his opinion that the operation should not take place at all.

Some of the deeper thinkers among the Wolseley Ring listened with close attention. They had kept their misgivings to themselves, but their private assessments had led them to the same conclusions as Buller's. The undertaking really had no proper military justification. The achievement of its objective would bring no conceivable strategic advantage. Its aims were the confused product of a woolly-minded humanitarianism, the deliverance of a self-centred idealist who had got himself into the mess that he was in simply because he had refused to do what he was told and of the party political needs of a vacillating, sanctimonious Prime Minister who had to placate an ill-informed voting public if he were to win the next general election for the Liberal party, a body not well thought of by the majority of Victorian senior officers.

Brave, bluff, inarticulate Buller, it seemed, was about to come into the open with these so far unexpressed reservations.

Wolseley asked Buller to elaborate upon the reasons behind his appreciation of the situation. Buller obliged in one sentence.

'The man's not worth the camels,' said Buller simply.

BEST NEWS IN YEARS

TO be able without controversy to name a town after your wife is an opportunity available to few modern men. In the British colony of Natal in South Africa the chance was given during the early nineteenth century to General Sir Harry Smith. With a Victorian distaste for exposing publicly the intimacies of his domestic nomenclature, he didn't call it after her Christian name. He called it Ladysmith.

As towns went, there was little to be said for it. It grew into a small, ugly agglomeration of dwellings and public buildings with corrugated iron roofs, grouped about a railway yard, and lying hotly in a dusty plain enclosed by low hills. As war with the Boers shifted from a possibility to imminence at the end of the 1890s, the railway sidings offered a useful facility for the establishment of a military supply base. When, in 1899, war broke out Ladysmith held a massive accumulation of stores.

The presence of these stores stood normal strategic thinking on its head. Instead of the stores being used to service the army on its operations, it became the aim of the army to protect the stores. In the pattern of where everyone and everything of relevance to both sides was at the outset of the campaign, Ladysmith was in the wrong place.

Strategic purists argued that the only sensible thing for the garrison to do was to destroy the stores, evacuate the town, and go south to a defensible position behind the Tugela river, there to unite with the reinforcements on their way from Britain. The garrison commander, General Sir George White ('That ass White': Field Marshal Sir Garnet Wolseley),

21

considered it to be his duty to stay where he was, a decision warmly seconded by the Governor of Natal, Sir Walter Hely-Hutchinson. The Governor felt that an abandonment would be bad for British prestige.

White's force fought and lost two chaotically conducted battles against the Boers in the countryside adjacent to Ladysmith, and then, in early November, withdrew to establish a defensive perimeter, fourteen miles long, around the town. Behind this, loosely surrounded by Boers, they settled down to await relief.

The relieving force, commanded by General Sir Redvers Buller ('Perhaps his mind is unhinged': Lord Lansdowne, Secretary of State for War), reached the Tugela shortly afterwards. Buller, who had left England in the belief that he had a range of strategic options open to him, found himself in practice restricted to one course only, the relief of Ladysmith. To achieve this it would be necessary to defeat, or to circumvent the Boers blocking his way on the far bank of the river.

Buller set about the task of clearing the blockage with spectacular ineptitude. He was aided by a former commandant of the Staff College, Lieutenant General Sir Francis Clery, an officer of arresting appearance who dyed his side-whiskers blue and was condemnatory of Boer behaviour ('Their tactics are never according to rule'); by Major-General Hart, who held the view that for troops in an assault to spread out was both unsoldierly and un-British, and by a broadly similar supporting cast.

Their preparations were hampered by Buller's miscalculation of the size of the Boer forces. In a signal to the War Office he estimated the total Boer armed strength to be 140,000 men, of whom 85,000 were from the Transvaal. 46,000 of these Transvaalers were, he said, either now in Natal or on the border, facing him. The reply came from Lord Lansdowne in person, who suggested that Buller might recheck his arithmetic. The entire white population of the Transvaal, male and female and including children, was 90,000.

Buller's force was still on the wrong side of the Tugela in late February. It had been defeated comprehensively at Colenso and at Spion Kop. Its fortunes were followed with concerned self-interest by the beleagured defenders of Ladysmith, who after nearly three months were becoming impatient.

The siege, although wearisome and debilitating, was in some ways a gentlemanly affair. There was no cause, as at Lucknow during the Indian Mutiny or at the more recent investment of the Peking legations in the course of the Boxer Rising, for the defenders to fight with desperation in the grim knowledge that defeat would equate with a barbarous death at the hands of the opposition.

The Boers cooperated in an arrangement by which those of the garrison's sick and wounded who were willing to go were taken to a hospital established behind the Boer lines. Shelling by Boer guns was desultory, inaccurate, and caused few casualties among soldiers and civilians who had early dug themselves shell-proof refuges. The Boers, as practising members of the Dutch Reformed Church, did not shoot on Sundays. As people of regular habits they fired their artillery on weekdays only between breakfast-time and dinner, with time off for lunch and tea.

These comforting peculiarities aside, they were in any case as puzzled about what to do next as General Buller was about what to do on the Tugela. The Boers were superb guerrilla fighters, but unaccustomed to siege warfare.

There was little serious fighting between besiegers and besieged. The Boers once overran British outpost positions on a couple of hills. The British took the hills back again. A raiding party from the garrison attacked and spiked one of the more troublesome Boer long-range guns.

The main difficulties of the defenders came from disease, boredom, dust, heat and hunger. The commonest diseases, their spread aggravated by poor diet and the sanitary inadequacies of the shell shelters, were dysentery and enteric. By February there were more than two thousand hospital cases, with a daily cluster of deaths. Those still on their feet showed the symptoms of weakness brought on by malnutrition. Cricket and amateur theatricals, popular during the early days of the siege, no longer had any following

23

whatsoever. The garrison endured and survived on hope.

The hope was raised, and as frequently lowered, by heliographed messages from Buller, struggling interminably about eight miles away on the Tugela. His coded forecasts of victories, followed by baffled admissions of defeats, were interlarded with *en clair* summaries of interesting news from the outside world, sent with intent to improve morale by giving the garrison something to talk about other than their own predicament. At the beginning of February, even this small source of solace became temporarily inoperative. Rain and cloud obscured the sun. The heliograph could not be used.

The break in communications added to the anxieties of the exhausted, undernourished defenders. It also led to an increase in speculation. Was Buller taking advantage of the bad weather to outwit the Boers? Low cloud and mist on Boer-defended hilltops would surely help a surprise attack, or allow Buller to slip part of his force through unseen. Talk about these possibilities was at its most intense when two days later the weather cleared. The sun came out. Within a few minutes the heliograph began to flash. Its message was awaited with controlled excitement.

It was brief, of one sentence only. 'SIR STAFFORD NORTHCOTE,' it read, 'GOVERNOR OF BOMBAY, HAS BEEN MADE A PEER.'

Encouraged by this glad news the garrison returned hungrily to work, at which it continued doggedly until the relief column finally broke through twenty-six days later.

Officer. 'WHAT THE DICKENS WAS THAT CALL YOU SOUNDED?'
Bugler. 'THE RALLY, SIR.'
Officer. 'I NEVER HEARD IT SOUNDED LIKE *THAT* BEFORE.'
Bugler. 'WELL, THAT'S 'OW THEY '*UMMED* IT TO ME!'

SMALL BOER MUSICAL SHOOTING

BRITISH tactical doctrine in 1899 was dominated by the experiences of the previous hundred years. The infantry square, which had frustrated the French at Waterloo, kept out Fuzzy Wuzzies and Afghans, and, although occasionally dented, had only been broken decisively once (by Zulus at Isandhlwana in circumstances judged to be almost unrepeatable) was still rehearsed as part of recruit training.

Steadiness of bearing, smartness of turnout, firm discipline and skill at moving in closely grouped tight formations, were considered by the traditionalists to be a sufficient basis for the preparation of the army to deal with any conceivable enemy. There were radical thinkers, impressed by contemporary developments in armaments production, who argued that times were changing fast and that the army would find itself in trouble if it didn't change with them. The influence of these advocates was limited. Their views did not widely prevail.

The Boers, when war was joined with them, early proved that the radicals were right and accelerated a British tactical revolution. Hardy backveldt mounted farmers, with an instinctive and inherited knowledge of fieldcraft and cross-country navigation in a countryside in which they had grown up, accustomed to using their wits in the ambush of food on the hoof, predators and inconvenient Africans, were equipped with modern German Mauser rifles that were accurate at long ranges and used smokeless cartridges. The Boers caused havoc among the slow-moving formalists who opposed them.

The British side made changes. It was no longer fashionably courageous to commit battalions, with bayonets fixed, to lumbering assaults upon hillsides manned by concealed marksmen who waited until the range was right and then, still concealed, massacred the attackers. The unlimbering of guns in exposed positions in which the crews and their horses were picked off methodically and in comfort by some of the finest rifle shots in the world was assessed as idiocy, not heroism. A tentative resort to flexibility, opportunism, cunning and a sensible disposition towards living to fight another day began to permeate through the more open-minded practitioners in the army.

One of these was Brigadier General Dixon of the 4th Infantry Brigade. When his command was caught off-balance by hidden Boers on a hill to the east of Kameelfontein Drift, the troops did not, as they might have done a few months previously, so group themselves as to furnish posthumous material for a member of the Royal Academy to paint an inspiring memorial to Dixon's Last Stand. The soldiers went smartly to ground. They exploited the available cover, and fought back.

It was a long hot day, with extensive two-way shooting. At the close of it, honours were about even. General Dixon, who throughout had prudently conducted his side of the proceedings in a prone attitude, rose to his feet when he considered that it was dark enough to do so in safety. He badly needed to stretch himself.

He looked around in the starlight, and was at once addressed by a nearby, invisible opponent.

'British can't catch Boer,' said this disembodied voice.

General Dixon did not reply.

The Boer burst into song. He gave the general Rule Britannia, tunefully, in an Afrikaner accent.

The general, still standing, made no comment.

The Boer, still in tune, word perfect, moved on to God Save the Queen. The general, made cautious by the new spirit of cunning that he was helping to promote, guessed what was coming next. For the first time in his military life he did not stand to attention for the national anthem. He dived to the ground, fast.

The Boer fired, missed, and laughed philosophically.

THE LOCATION OF THE HEART

WHETHER the origins of the ritual lay on the terraces of football stadiums, in Edwardian music halls or on the pantomime stage, is open to discussion and research. The most likely of the three is that it came from that part of a pantomime in which the principal boy resorts to consultation with the audience about the baddies.

'They've gone away, haven't they?'

'NO-O-O-OH.'

'Will I kill them?'

'YE-E-ESS.'

The military variant, widely in vogue for most of the First World War, less so in some of the Second, involved, as in pantomime, a solo putter of a question with a known answer and a roared chorused reply.

'Are we downhearted?'

'NO-O-O-OH.'

Troops on tedious working parties, marching at ease or simply sitting about and smoking, drew comfort and reassurance from the reiteration of this simple dialogue. Officers and senior NCOs would not risk making themselves ridiculous by instigating it, but were always glad to hear it. It was an earnest of a determination not to bend before adversity, an indication that morale remained sound in the face of hardships, dangers and irritations.

The officers of an infantry battalion on the last stage of their journey to reinforce the expedition to Gallipoli in 1915 were heartened when the familiar shouted chant echoed from the decks of the converted cargo ship in which they were approaching the peninsula. It was clear from all reports that the fighting on the beaches and among the hills and gullies had been savage. Casualties, eventually to total 205,000 killed, deaths from sickness and injury, had already been enormous.

On this velvet, still, moonlit, starlit, Mediterranean summer's night, the decks were crowded with unsleeping soldiers, talking quietly, looking at the spasmodic flashes of gunfire from the land ahead of them.

Visibility was good enough to let them see another steamer approaching them a long way away on a nearly reciprocal course. When it came nearer they identified it as a hospital ship. It passed close by, to starboard. When it was level an enthusiastic voice cut across the subdued babble of chatter on the transport.

'Are we downhearted?'

'NO-O-O-OOH,' bawled several hundred men on the way to the loss of their military virginity.

An unscheduled third line came clearly across the sea from the hospital ship. It was delivered sardonically, in an Australian accent. 'Well if you're not now,' said this realist, 'you bloody soon will be.'

RALLY TO THE COLOURS

UPLIFTED by reports of an occasion when the leader of an attack mounted by the London Scottish at Neuve Chapelle had punted a football ahead of him to give encouragement to his men and introduce an element of unusual interest to the undertaking, the editor of a London newspaper in 1915 instructed his correspondent in France to write a series. It was to be about the use of similar eccentric adjuncts to leadership in battle, and about who used them.

It would be a natural, said the editor. The readership would love it. Real-life illustrations of the British capacity to rise to the occasion, leaven heroism with humour, adapt tradition and sporting skills to the conditions of war, demonstrate the national individuality, that sort of thing.

The correspondent sought assistance from the press officer at GHQ, who was helpful. The press officer did some research, made some inquiries, and handed over a list of likely candidates for inclusion in the series. There was a minor problem about most of them, he said. They weren't available for interview. One was dead, some were wounded, two were on leave in England, and the others were either too busy with their units in the Line or too shy to be willing to talk to a newspaper. There was, however, a rich body of material on file about each. Why didn't the correspondent base his articles on that? The press officer would continue to scratch around to see if at least one or two personal interviews could be arranged.

This suited the correspondent. It cut down on the work. Whatever he wrote would be minced into some form of propaganda, distorted in the interests of circulation figures

30

and patriotic emotionalism. He settled down to sift through the material.

There seemed to be a surprising number of officers who went into action blowing hunting horns, bagpipes and bugles, and one oddity who did so whilst playing a saxophone. There were those who waved hunting crops, others with imperial ancestors or experience who brandished knobkerries, scimitars and battle axes, a former Wimbledon contender who carried a tennis racket and belted over unstoppable services from the middle of No-Man's-Land, and a golfer with a mashie-niblick who teed up in front of his company and drove balls over the German wire.

This was all useful grist to the journalistic mill and was written up, with trimmings. One star turn in this *galère*, the press officer said after further inquiries, was actually both willing to be interviewed and currently out of the Line. He was a major named Pryor, the second-in-command of a battalion of a Home Counties regiment. Pryor's speciality during an attack was to wear his grandfather's tunic. His grandfather had been a Victorian general, and the tunic was scarlet.

The press officer arranged a meeting and provided transport. The correspondent was driven to a farmhouse, now in use as battalion headquarters.

Major Pryor turned out not to be one of those reticent heroes who shrug modestly with an embarrassed smile when asked about their exploits. He was an eloquently obsessive megalomaniac with a flair for stage management. Instead of the quiet question and answer session over a cup of coffee or a drink that the correspondent had expected, there was something approaching a *son et lumiére* display. Pryor, wearing the famed scarlet tunic, regulation riding breeches and field boots, had a demonstration platoon in full marching order lined up behind him. Their embittered expressions suggested that some time had already been spent upon rehearsal. Pryor shook hands brusquely and got straight down to business.

'Now,' he said resonantly, 'I have devised this presentation to illustrate the advantages that follow upon an officer of my seniority dressing as I do in a battalion assault. In essence,

31

they are two. The first is control. Some confusion in action is inevitable. I minimize it. I provide a rallying point, an inspiration. Its central ingredient is visibility. Anyone temporarily lost, or unsure of what to do, has only to look around, identify my red coat, and be reassured. If in doubt he can come to me for orders.'

Pryor paused, and stared dramatically at the demonstration platoon. They stared resignedly back.

Mounted Officer. 'AW—ARE YOU THE WEST RIDING?'
Voice from the Ranks. NO! WE'RE THE BLOOMIN' BUFFS—*WALKIN'*!'

'You may well ask,' continued Pryor, looking at the correspondent with a challenging scowl, 'you may well ask: If the second-in-command is so conspicuously visible to his own men, is he not equally conspicuously visible to the Germans? Will they not concentrate their fire on him? The answer to that question is Yes. Of course they will. I expect it.' He lowered his voice grimly. 'But that,' he said, emphasizing each word like a slow succession of gun shots, 'is-what-I-am-paid-for.'

His decible output came back to normal. 'And now,' he cried, 'for part one of the presentation. Sergeant Smith.'

Sergeant Smith called the platoon to attention, and marched them off wearily in fours to a neighbouring muddy field. They spread out into extended order, and waited. Pryor took up a position forty yards ahead of them. He blew a whistle. They all advanced, Pryor in front in his scarlet jacket, the troops plodding behind with rifles, bayonets fixed, held at the high port.

Pryor blew his whistle again. They halted. Pryor turned towards them.

'Sergeant Smith,' bawled Pryor, 'can you see me?'

'Yes, sir,' shouted Sergeant Smith.

'You there, right-hand man. Can you see me?'

'Yes, sir.'

'Left-hand man. Can you?'

'With total clarity,' said the left-hand man unexpectedly. He had a cultivated, sardonic voice.

Pryor stared at him briefly, gave it up, and told Sergeant Smith to march the platoon back to the farmyard. There, they were ordered to stand easy. Pryor braced his legs in front of them and flexed his swagger cane.

'You will appreciate,' rasped Pryor to the correspondent, 'that it is impossible to simulate battle conditions with precision. That was only an approximation. It should however have given you some idea of the value to troops of the presence of a readily identifiable senior officer to whom they can turn when under pressure.'

Pryor, who seemed to be expecting some form of endorsement, or admiring comment, stared fixedly into the correspondent's eyes. The correspondent nodded nervously, wondering how to get away from this lunatic.

'Now,' said Pryor, 'I said earlier that there were *two* benefits that arise from my wearing a scarlet jacket. The first, visibility, you have seen demonstrated. The second, more incalculable, concerns that elusive, essential, indefinable quality, morale. The men may not realize it,' – he turned to gaze at them with paternal sympathy – 'but if senior officers are wounded in action they bleed just like anyone else. A senior officer who is hit and is seen to bleed, for that matter a senior officer who shows external signs of any physical weakness whatsoever, is one with a bad effect on morale, HE BECOMES A LIABILITY. Men who rely upon him for leadership and guidance, who draw confidence from his presence, may lose heart if they see him stained with his own blood.'

Pryor glowered again at the correspondent. The correspondent gave a repeat performance of his nervous nod.

'You see what I am getting at,' went on Pryor, spelling it out. '*My* tunic is the same colour as my blood. *My* tunic does *not* show blood.'

He accentuated the intensity of his mesmeric stare upon the correspondent. The owner of the voice from the demonstration platoon was never officially identified, but the correspondent was later prepared to put his money on the man who in the muddy field had seen Pryor with total clarity.

'You will also notice,' said this commentator, 'that he wears khaki riding breeches.'

BREAD UPON THE WATERS

THE only soldier in the long history of the British army to have held every rank from trooper to field marshal was Sir William Robertson. He started his working life as a boy servant in the household of Lord Cardigan, the hero of Balaclava or the idiot who lost the Light Brigade, depending upon which way you look at it. Neither contact with this querulous peer nor pathetic appeals from his mother deterred the young Robertson from enlistment.

In view of the professional and social obstacles that he had to get over or past in the course of his rise to distinction it is not a surprise that he was known as a dour man, not given to the delivery of off-the-cuff witticisms. He did, however, make a joke in 1917. The records suggest that it was his only one.

He was Chief of the Imperial General Staff at the time. It was the era when the higher direction of the First World War was soured by bitter disagreement between Frocks and Brasshats, the politicians of the war cabinet and the professional leaders of the army. Mistrust, suspicion, contempt and accusations of incapacity flowered on both sides of the divide.

In a high gale on a winter's day, Robertson embarked on a destroyer at Dover, and headed towards General Headquarters in France where he was to confer with General Sir Douglas Haig, the commander-in-chief. With Robertson was Lord Rhondda, a Frock of note, recently appointed by Mr Lloyd George to coordinate arrangements for the distribution of the nation's food supplies. Lord Rhondda's official designation was a succinct one. He was called the food controller.

As the cross-Channel journey progressed the gale blew harder. The destroyer bucketed about disconcertingly. Robertson was a good sailor. Lord Rhondda was not. He redistributed his lunch, at intervals, in spasms.

Robertson struck a blow for his side in the Brass-hat – Frock controversy.

'Rhondda,' said Robertson, as Rhondda wiped the sweat from his face after about his sixth regurgitation, 'you don't seem to *me* to be much of a food controller.'

PASTORAL STATE OF ALERT

THE campaign conducted by General Sir Edmund Allenby against the Turks in Palestine in 1917 was notable for its skilful planning, sound organization, unsparing attention to detail and the taking of calculated risks. It was a famous victory, and it provoked much discussion among those struggling in the more pedestrian conditions of France and Flanders on the Western Front. There were earnest searches for lessons learnt in the Near East that could be adapted to conditions in the West, and there was admiration and a certain amount of envy for all that mobility and room to move in.

In the course of one of these informal reviews of Palestinian developments, held in a headquarters mess in which an old tradition had been discarded and where it was now respectable to talk shop, the emphasis was shifted temporarily from an erudite analysis of strategy and tactics to something of less immediacy but, as the man who shifted it said, of lasting historical and theological significance.

Did everyone present, asked the padre, appreciate the importance to Christendom and to Western civilization of the fact that the Australians had captured Bethlehem? This feat would stand out long after the military urgencies of the moment had been forgotten. The Australians had achieved more than the Crusaders ever had, and that no other Christian force had ever achieved either. For the first time since the Islamic defeat of Byzantium centuries before, the birthplace of Our Lord was in Christian hands.

There was a show of polite, patient enthusiasm for this

37

aspect of affairs, coupled to an urge to get back to the main subject under discussion. The padre was insensitive to these undercurrents. He became eloquent with some confused, exalted stuff about spiritual rejuvenation, and the future need to mount a perpetual watch upon a newly recovered Christian shrine, on all the other holy places in Palestine, and on any other former Christian assets once sequestrated by the Ottoman Empire but now within range of repossession.

Some way through this homily a late arrival joined the group. He was a lieutenant colonel who had thought that he had come to talk about something different from what the padre was talking about, but he listened with close attention.

'Who did you say has taken Bethlehem?' he asked, when he could get a word in.

'The Australians,' answered the padre.

The colonel looked thoughtful. He was thinking of a past experience of his when he had fought alongside an Australian infantry battalion. He had then been full of admiration for their qualities in action but less so of their habits out of it. They were known as the Forty Thieves.

'If the Australians are in Bethlehem,' said the colonel, 'then the shepherds *better* watch their bloody flocks by night.'

A ROSE IS A ROSE, BUT WHAT'S THAT OTHER STUFF?

MR Robert Graves, who should know, because he was a front-line officer with the Royal Welch Fusiliers in France in the 1914–18 war and once wrote a book subtitled 'The future of Swearing and Improper Language', put forward an interesting theory about the manner in which the use of Anglo-Saxon four-letter words and their grammatical variations became tolerated and then fashionable among the British ruling classes in the early part of the twentieth century. Mr Graves attributed it largely to the First World War.

His argument was that, traditionally, British nobs and British plebs exchanged little in the way of words except when the first gave instructions to the second and the second acknowledged them. These ritualistic occasions aside, neither of the parties had much idea of the sentence patterns of the other. It was the daily propinquity of trench life in France and Flanders that changed all this. For the first time in British history everybody began to understand what everybody else said and to recognize how they said it.

Every rule has its exceptions, and some rules have several. One of the exceptions to Graves' Rule was a general, a member of the ruling classes if ever there was one, who commanded at Ahmednagar in India in the early 1900s. General Dale either had undisclosed linguistic resources of his own or had been hobnobbing with the lower orders to an extent unusual in an officer of his age and station. Whatever the seam was that he drew upon, it was rich, unadulterated by circumlocutions, and would have been more familiar to Hengist and Horsa than to Mr Bowdler and Queen Victoria.

Despite the absence of inhibition with which he distributed his monosyllables, General Dale subscribed to one convention of his day. He applied a scrupulous self-censorship when women were present. It had been believed widely that this practice of his was of universal application, until evidence from the general's quarters suggested that his wife might be excepted from it.

Mrs Dale, as the wife of the area commander, held social responsibilities. She was the arbiter of what was done and of what was not done by the wives and daughters of officers. She kept a distant, motherly eye upon the wives and families of the NCOs and, in the few cases where they existed, those of the private soldiers. At dinners, balls, race meetings and all other examples of formal relaxation, she took precedence over every other woman present other than the wife of the civil deputy commissioner. She carried out these duties conscientiously and well. She was a little austere, and a little detached, but these qualities were expected of a general's wife in India in the early years of the reign of King Edward the seventh.

Mrs Dale, however, was not one of those army wives so dedicated to the addition of domestic and social decoration to their husbands' careers that they abandon any private life of their own. There wasn't much for a feminine individualist to do in a place like Ahmednagar, but what there was was done by Mrs Dale. She painted in water colours. She practised for hours on end at the piano. She was tireless in supervising the cultivation of her garden. And she sought and enjoyed the company of interesting people, missionaries, teachers, Box Wallahs' wives and the like, not customarily included on the visiting list of a general's wife operating in the hierarchical exclusiveness of Edwardian India.

One of these, to her husband's mind, strange friends was a member of the Christian Missionary Society. Her name was Miss Pringle, and she embodied to an extraordinary degree the amalgam of selflessness, devotion, adventurousness, knowledgeability about India and the Indians, spiritual pride and the prudishness that at the same time was characteristic of many of her profession.

Miss Pringle's daily work had for twenty years taken her among the sights, smells, and sounds of an impoverished society indifferent to the disciplines of elementary sanitation, and in which neither the visual arts nor the obligations of religious practice were reticent about bodily appurtenances, functions and peculiarities. She seemed somehow to have reached an accommodation with all this, without in any way letting it disturb a rigidly Victorian puritanism. Miss Pringle might know all about it, but there were things that were not said to Miss Pringle.

She was invited frequently to tea by Mrs Dale, and more than paid for the hospitality by enriching Mrs Dale's store of knowledge about Indian history, customs, music, poetry, flora and fauna. Mrs Dale was interested in all of these, but was particularly fascinated by Miss Pringle's familiarity with the local techniques of growing flowers.

After an unusually helpful contribution of Miss Pringle's upon this subject, Mrs Dale took her on a tour of her own garden. Miss Pringle examined appreciatively the chrysanthemums, the riotous blaze of Canna lilies, the brilliant orange of the marigolds, the white waxy blossoms of the frangipani, the pink hibiscus and the deep crimson poinsettia. Miss Pringle, with an expression of pure pleasure, said that she was both delighted and impressed. It was the most beautiful garden that she had seen for years. What was Mrs Dale's secret?

'Manure,' said Mrs Dale simply. 'Lots and lots of manure.'

Miss Pringle's face changed at once. She frowned, pursed her lips, and looked primly disapproving. Mrs Dale might be a general's wife and Miss Pringle's social superior and hostess, but Miss Pringle was not prepared to tolerate this sort of vulgarity.

'I have always preferred to call it fertilizer,' said Miss Pringle coldly.

Village Clergyman. 'CAN I HELP YOU AT ALL?' *Artilleryman.* 'YES, SIR, YOU CAN.'
Clergyman. 'WHAT SHALL I DO, THEN?'
Artilleryman. 'WELL, SIR, IF YOU WOULDN'T MIND GOING A BIT FURTHER UP THE STREET THE HORSES WILL UNDERSTAND THE LANGUAGE BETTER.'

'Well, for God's sake don't tell the general that,' said Mrs Dale. 'It's taken me twenty-five years to get him to call it manure.'

AN ENGLISHMAN'S WORD

IN some Indian cities some collective tempers become short during the hot weather. In the early part of this century, before the subcontinent had divided into predominantly Hindu India and predominantly Muslim Pakistan, large cohesive communities of followers of both religions lived in many cities. When it became monotonously hot, and particularly if the hotness coincided with the Muslim fasting month of Ramadhan when abstention from food and drink during daylight hours promoted a general irritability in any case, people were prone to brood upon grievances. The most common grievances were to do with the intolerably provocative, unclean, patronizing, selfish, inconsiderate, heretical etc. characteristics of members of the religion to which the brooders did not subscribe. When the brooding was translated into an urge towards taking practical remedial action, the annual rioting season was beginning to get under way.

Those responsible for preserving the peace then brought into motion a well-tried sequence, any step of which might, or might not, close down hostilities for the current year.

(1) The civil authorities, the deputy commissioner or his representatives, appealed to community leaders to advise their coreligionists to calm down.
(2) If (1) got nowhere, the police became ostentatiously active. They patrolled intercommunal boundaries, issued warnings to be of good behaviour, and arrested a few of the persistently belligerent.
(3) Should enthusiasm for getting to grips with the other side

43

continue to increase, police riot squads appeared upon the streets. The presence of the riot squads could, with luck, end the difficulty. Without the luck, the riot squads were likely to be attacked by delegations from both communities.

(4) At this point it was time for the military to be called in to perform the least popular of its many roles, that of Aid to the Civil Power. Two simple alternative consequences were attendant upon these duties. If the army shot a rioter or two, dispersed the mobs, and by so doing saved scores of lives and prevented the destruction of much property, some of it sacred, the soldiers were accused by Indian and British politicians, commentators and polemicists of callous brutality. If they failed to restore order, the accusations were of weakness, inefficiency and, sometimes, of cowardice.

(5) The troops marched stolidly to where the excitement was at its most pronounced, halted, and faced the crowd. A magistrate, as often as not operating under an intermittent bombardment from stones, bricks, and garbage, read the Riot Act. The Riot Act gave legality to what could, but it was hoped wouldn't, happen next. If the mob failed to go away peacefully, the magistrate warned them, the soldiers would open fire.

(6) Often the crowd went home, complaining. Sometimes it didn't. If it didn't the officer commanding the troops selected one of the noisier ringleaders, identified him clearly to the best marksman available, and ordered the marksman to shoot him. Experience had demonstrated the unwisdom of taking a seemingly more humane option, the firing of shots over the crowd's head to frighten it into dispersal. All shots land somewhere. Too many, when this expedient had been tried, had caused the deaths of distant innocent people, followed by justified anger and grief.

(7) After a ringleader, perhaps two or three ringleaders, had been shot the crowd would break up, sometimes to re-form later, usually not. When the last act of this year's version of a recurrent performance was over, the troops returned to barracks, the police resumed normal policing, everyday life carried on much as before, and the deputy commissioner, the

police superintendent and the senior military commander allowed themselves some modest self-congratulation upon the proposition that an incalculable, but heavy, loss of life had been prevented by the taking of those of a few.

In April 1919, occurrences in the Jallianwala Bag in Amritsar, the Sikh holy city in the Punjab, affected the manner in which subsequent Indian urban riots were dealt with. The Amritsar trouble shifted from rhetoric to violence after the deportation of two more than averagely fierce Sikh leaders. An avenging crowd, heading for the deputy commissioner's house, refused to turn back but was forced to do so when the picquet guarding the house opened fire. Rioting spread, fast. The town hall and two banks were burned, the telegraph office was attacked, one of the bank managers and his assistant were beaten to death, a European engineer and an Indian railway guard were also murdered and a European woman missionary was thrashed into unconsciousness and left for dead. The situation soon moved beyond the capacity of the police to contain it. Control was handed to the military.

General Dyer was in command. He chose to undertake his duties not by delegation through the command structure, but in person. When a large crowd of angry demonstrators, assembled in the enclosed space of the Jallianwala Bag, refused to disperse, General Dyer ordered the Gurkha troops with him to open fire. There was none of the target selectivity that was a normal feature of such orders. The intensity of the ensuing massacre was compounded because any orders to cease fire were unheard in the overpowering noise, and because available escape routes, left open customarily as a matter of commonsense tactics when forcible crowd control became necessary, were on this occasion blocked. Nearly four hundred people were killed and many more injured. Dyer was widely condemned as a ruthless butcher,* and was sacked.

* There's little to be said for General Dyer, although he had defenders at the time, by no means all mindless blood-crazed zealots, who argued that if he'd been any less lethally destructive the whole of the Punjab would have been exposed to an anarchy that would have cost many times the number of lives

The sacking did not close the controversy. Accusations that the Government of India in New Delhi, and the Imperial Government in London, had sponsored, or at its lowest, condoned an atrocity were bitter and widespread. The accusers included many who had previously been politically uncommitted, as well as the predictable genuine idealists and the less genuine opportunists with potentially profitable fingers in the political pie.

Amritsar became a symbol of significance, its name a rallying cry in the movement towards Indian independence. Its influence was felt as far away as Ireland, where British troops at the time, resignedly aiding yet another Civil Power, were helping to try to inhibit a progression that was to lead to the establishment of the Irish Free State in 1922. Some of the more simple-minded fire-eating military commanders, tempted to take out their frustrations upon uncooperative assemblies of non-combatants, were held back by injunctions to avoid another Amritsar; an injunction that was usually effective with the soldiers, but regrettably not with the Auxiliaries and Black and Tans, temporary policemen, whose excesses were to the prolonged detriment of Anglo-Irish relations.

One of the many consequences of the Amritsar shootings in India itself was that the civil and military authorities took a close look at their riot control procedures. Caution was clearly advisable if what in the past had been almost routine restorations of the public peace were not to develop, probably helped along by some artificial exploitation, into major political propaganda disasters. In at least one area a wise exercise of caution was replaced by an unwise resort to over-

lost in Amritsar. These supporters opened a fund to sustain him in his premature retirement. It was very well supported. It is of relevance in judging Dyer that when in 1984 the independent government of India, with Mrs Gandhi in the chair, was confronted by similar Sikh dissidence in Amritsar, Indian troops using automatic weapons put in an attack that killed more Sikhs than Dyer did, violated the sacredness of the Sikh temple, and according to reported medical evidence, was followed by the shooting of bound prisoners.

caution. Orders passed down through the layers of the hierarchy to the man who would have to carry them out left him with a feeling of mixed loneliness and vulnerability.

Such a man was a company commander among whose internal security tasks was riot control in a city with a population of differing religions and volatile habits. His standing orders were redrafted with much nit-picking attention to the dictionary definition of indivual words, and to the accurate placing of commas and full stops. What it all added up to was that should a danger of a serious breach of the peace arise he was authorized to threaten to respond with force but was in no circumstances to use it.

He was not a man of a notably reflective disposition, but it didn't take him long to work out the implications of this. He presented himself at battalion headquarters and asked the adjutant for a translation into the vernacular.

'What it means,' he was told, 'is that when they start throwing things about, and you're called in, you march your lads to the scene of the trouble and stand there, looking intimidating. If that doesn't work, and it goes on getting worse, you threaten to open fire unless it gets better again. And if that doesn't work either, you don't do anything.'

'Thanks,' said the company commander. 'Thanks a lot. What happens then? I mean if it just goes on getting worse.'

'If it looks as though you'll have casualties, you withdraw with dignity.'

'Just bugger off?'

'With dignity.'

'Who drafted this bollocks?'

'Not me,' said the adjutant, 'someone much closer to God.'

'Well, bloody good,' said the company commander, 'I can see happy times ahead.'

Three weeks later he stood, a platoon of his company formed up behind him, facing an agitated mob who were intent upon the incineration of a mosque. Another rival mob was to his rear, deployed to defend the mosque. The police had done what they could, but things by now were well beyond their control. A gazetted magistrate had formally read the Riot Act. Bits of brick were flying about. There were spasmodic embittered shouts. It was time for the company commander to implement the first part of his orders.

He told a soldier, with as much ostentation as possible, to load with a five-round clip of .303 ammunition. He pointed with his swagger stick to the most prominent and noisy leader of the crowd. He addressed the leader in careful, loud Hindustani.

'I am acting under orders,' said the company commander, in a steady, spuriously steely voice. 'Unless you advise your followers to disperse, peaceably and at once, you will take the consequences.'

He nodded to the chosen rifle shot, who raised his gun unwaveringly. Its muzzle pointed at the crowd-leader's forehead, sights fixed on a point an inch above the gap between his eyebrows. The range was about twelve yards.

The crowd-leader, who was no keener on suicide than anyone else, was none the less a brave man, at a high pitch of religious exaltation. There was also the saving of face to consider. He flinched, but he spoke out firmly, conscious of an attentive audience behind him.

'Suppose,' he said, 'that I say No.'

'Then,' said the company commander ferociously, 'I will carry out the second part of my orders.'

The crowd didn't break up as quickly and as quietly as was altogether desirable, but it left.

MARTIAL SPIRIT

DURING the years immediately following the First World War there was a surge of interest in spiritualism. The death roll had been huge. Many bereaved relatives tried to establish contact with their dead menfolk.

In Edinburgh, five Scottish war widows experimented independently of one another. They tried table-tapping, Ouija boards and thought transmission. A number of professional charlatans who claimed psychic powers gave themselves names like Madame Brahmaputra and charged through the nose for chanting gibberish from behind veils, under dimmed lights and to a pervading smell of incense. None of these ventures was successful.

Through separate friends the ladies were pointed towards a medium called Jeannie. The simplicity of her name was as reassuring as was her appearance. Jeannie was a plump, comfortable middle-aged woman who dressed in tweeds and flat shoes and who operated without ostentation from the sitting room of a modest suburban house. There was no bogus exotic flim-flam about Jeannie.

Her arrangements, too, were sensible. After the five individual approaches had been made to her by the widows, she invited them all to attend at her house at four o'clock on a Wednesday afternoon. Introductions were made, tea and biscuits were distributed and Jeannie explained her ground rules. There would be a businesslike small charge to cover the tea and biscuits, contribute to heating and lighting bills and help pay for the cleaning woman. Otherwise Jeannie's services were free. She had the gift, but had done nothing to earn it. It simply possessed her mysteriously. It would be wrong to profit from it.

It was necessary, said Jeannie briskly, for the ladies to understand how things worked. Different mediums had different capabilities. In her case she was able, sometimes after preliminary difficulties about identification, to set up two-way communications between originators of messages on earth and recipients in the Hereafter. Her own role was that of a conduit. She could hear both ends of a conversation, and would repeat conscientiously to earth what came down from above, and vice versa, but she had no control over what was said. They should think of her as a relay station, reporting verbatim.

'And now,' said Jeannie, 'let's try and see what happens.'

It was all very matter-of-fact. By the end of the afternoon all the ladies were in touch with their late husbands. Any doubts that it might be a cruel, elaborate trick were put to rest by Jeannie's insistence that authenticity should be confirmed by references to domestic matters that could only be known to the communicating parties. Inquiries from above about whether the chimney still smoked when the wind was in the northwest, and reminders to check the lagging on the cistern pipes before winter frosts arrived were clinchers.

At six o'clock Jeannie called a halt. The ladies were very moved, but happy, and Jeannie was worn out. She suggested, and they agreed, that they must try not to overdo it. If the high standard of transmission were to be maintained they should discipline themselves to, say, two hours a week. Why not every Wednesday at the same time? There was general concurrence. The widows paid their contributions to the overheads and left.

For the next eight Wednesdays the Ground-to-Hereafter system flourished. Jeannie exhausted herself in repeating chatty messages in either direction. On the tenth Wednesday she found the traffic slightly less demanding. By the twelfth, there were actually a few awkward silences. It seemed to Jeannie that some familiar terrestrial patterns were redeveloping. Husbands and wives were beginning to run out of conversation. A touch of boredom was creeping in.

The trouble started on the fifteenth Wednesday. It arose in the context of one of the indicators that had earlier been so useful in establishing Jeannie's credentials. An admittedly rather thoughtlessly worded contribution from below drew a long, sullen silence from above. This was followed by irritated comment upon the lagging on the cistern. The message from above was that the sender knew damned well that his reminder had not been heeded, that the pipes had burst, that much damage had been done, and that yet again unnecessary expense had been incurred because of lack of forethought, failure to pay attention and general incompetence.

A swift riposte went straight back through Jeannie. If her husband wanted to start that kind of stuff, said the lady, there were a few bits of unfinished business that he might like to account for. Who was it who in 1913 let the Sunday roast burn to a cinder while she herself was at church? Who was responsible for the destruction of a glass panel in the kitchen door because he was too lazy to lock it properly at a time when it was obvious to anyone but an idiot that a gale was blowing up? And what about his persistently filthy habit of not removing his boots when he came in from the garden, thereby ruining the carpets.

For a short time there was seething quiet above. Jeannie was able to relax a little. Then, another voice came down. An astral alliance had clearly formed hastily. The fresh intervention was from a husband who asked sarcastically whether his relict was still carrying on with that yellow git of a conscientious objector from the bank. A counter-punch of: 'You needn't think I didn't know about you and Nellie Hunter,' was nearly crowded off the air by a further recollection of the first widow. She drew attention to a bicycle that had been damaged beyond repair when her husband fell off it, drunk, while returning from an international Soccer match.

Amidst hotly phrased responses from above, and something new from below about somebody who had lied about the true size of his wage packet and had cheated on his allocation of housekeeping money, Jeannie switched off. Like a telephone exchange at a time of crisis she had become overloaded. She was also very cross.

She gave the ladies a stern dressing-down. She had, she said, put her unusual gift at their disposal, free of charge, at considerable personal inconvenience and at considerable personal wear and tear, in order as she thought to help them. For the first few weeks she had thought that she *had* helped them. But if there was to be no more to it than a lot of unpleasant post-marital bickering she intended to have nothing further to do with it. Either they would undertake to behave themselves in future, or there would be no more séances.

The ladies were chastened. They apologized and gave the undertaking. They assembled on the following Wednesday looking contrite, subdued and embarrassed. Jeannie loosened them up over the tea and biscuits, and then opened up communications.

There was no reply. The husbands above, without Jeannie to keep them in order, were obviously united in a sulky solidarity. The ladies below became increasingly uneasy. Jeannie, restored to sympathy with them, told them not to despair. There was still one course open to them. Contact could be made with a messenger above, known personally to all five husbands. He could then be asked to make representations. Could the ladies think of a fellow-dead soldier who had known all five to do the job?

Prolonged consultation provided no names. The husbands had served in different regiments, or in two cases in different battalions of the same regiment. They had all been killed at different times. So far as was known there had been no friend common to all of them.

The ladies were about to give up, when one of them made a suggestion. They would all have seen, she said, recent newspaper reports about the ceremonial burial in Westminster Abbey of the Unknown Warrior. An unidentified body had been disinterred in Flanders, brought to London and buried with full military honours in the nave of the abbey in the presence of King George V. The Unknown Warrior represented those thousands, possibly hundreds of thousands, of Allied battle casualties who had died in similar circumstances, honoured but beyond recognition. His status presumably gave him a wide circle of acquaintanceship above. Why didn't Jeannie try to enlist him as a conciliator? Jeannie said that she would.

She worked at it in deep concentration. After several false starts she was almost sure that she was through, but there was a difficulty. The Unknown Warrior, if that was who it was, was speaking in a foreign language. Jeannie spoke no foreign languages, not even schoolgirl French.

One of the ladies was fluent in French. She wrote out in translation Jeannie's inquiry of: 'Are you the Unknown Warrior?' Jeannie tried several times, but was unable to master the pronunciation. She thought of a new tack. It might work, she said, if the French speaker held both of Jeannie's hands, put the question herself, and used Jeannie as the transmitting channel.

They positioned themselves. Jeannie nodded. The French speaker said slowly and clearly: '*Est ce que vous êtes le soldat inconnu qui dorme dans l'abbaye de Westminster?*'

There was an immediate response.

'*Jawohl*,' said the Unknown Warrior.

The Pess-Optimist. 'WOT A LIFE! NO REST, NO BEER, NO NUFFIN. IT'S ONLY US KEEPING SO CHEERFUL AS PULLS US THROUGH!'

53

HORSE WITH EMOTION

THE retrospective judgement of most members of the
syndicate was that the thing first began to get out of
hand when Molly Bastin was enlisted by her husband
to plug the sale of shares.

Until she started clouding the issue by the introduction of
unethical techniques into what should have been straightforward commercial transactions, everything had been
comfortably under control. Purchasers had come in with their
eyes open. They had made their own assessments of the risks,
recognized the potential for high profits, and accepted
unemotionally the possibility of loss, which they were
equipped financially to write off.

The shareholders introduced by Molly were neither knowledgeable nor dispassionate. Some of them may have thought
that they were knowledgeable, but what they really were was
passionate. Molly talking about the virtues of a horse was
always informative and interesting, but Molly doing so while
showing a lot of stockinged leg, casually exposing a hint of
cleavage, and emitting gusts of Chanel No. 5, was irresistible.
The quality of the horse, undisputed in this case, became
secondary to unrequited lust. All sorts of suckers, notably
twenty-five gentlemen cadets from the Royal Military
Academy, Woolwich, signed on who shouldn't. They couldn't
afford it if matters went wrong.

The horse was a filly named Delgany Girl. Bastin, Molly's
husband, had first set eyes on her when he went to Ireland for
a veterinary symposium. Looking back on it all later the
purists in the syndicate, cavalry officers and Guardees and a

couple of horsily inclined naval officers from the Home Fleet, considered that an unwritten prospectus founded upon the letting loose of someone like Bastin in a place like Ireland might reasonably have been examined a little more carefully than it had been.

Bastin was an Australian major in the Royal Army Veterinary Corps, to which, unusually, he had come by personal invitation. He had attracted the attention of General Sir Edmund Allenby during the general's drive on Gaza in his campaign against the Turks in Palestine in 1917. Bastin had been with the Australian Light Horse. In the prevention and cure of equine ailments and injuries he had shown himself to be a near genius, a qualified practitioner who soared far above the prescriptions of his professional training into heights of intuitive diagnosis and startlingly successful remedial unorthodoxy. Bastin's rapport with horses was instinctive and total. His admirers said that he was practically a horse himself.

General Allenby, once the commander of the Cavalry Division, the last operational leader in British military history to use mounted troops in quantity in a winning campaign, had relied upon the dash and skill of his cavalry to circumvent the Turks. At the end of what had been a punishing test of endurance for man and beast, he inspected the Australian Light Horse. He was impressed beyond measure when he saw the fruits of their high standard of animal management. Their colonel gave most of the credit to Bastin.

Allenby had a long talk with Bastin and suggested that if he wanted to make his career in the British army after the war he, Allenby, would sponsor him. Bastin accepted.

An Allenby recommendation was the equivalent of a first-class ticket. In 1919 Bastin was duly transferred, while retaining his existing seniority, to the Royal Army Veterinary Corps. In this new ambience he earned top marks for professional competence and devotion, and generated some snobbish disdain for his cheerful indifference to the social niceties as honoured in peacetime by a still notably class-sensitive regular army. Both Bastin and his young bride,

Molly, were slapdash about leaving cards and returning calls. They were seriously unrepentant about their vowels. In his off-duty moments he wore suits of loud check and flashy ties. She wore unsuitable dresses that showed more of her than was customary in Aldershot.

Bastin's extramural preoccupations were also the subject of much comment, some unfavourable, some not. A natural born gambler, sired by distinguished Australian betting stock, he became the scourge of the British bookies. Part of his success derived from his affinity with horses. There were those who suspected that a few of his *coups* owed a lot to inside information from sources not above the manipulation of results to guarantee a sound financial return to bent trainers and jockeys. Bastin was not choosy about the company he kept. Criticism on this count was modified by the generosity with which Bastin passed on reliable tips to whoever asked for them.

It was 1925 before his winnings had accumulated to a sufficient size to allow him to be confident about setting himself up as an owner. There was recurrent as well as capital expense to bear in mind. His original intention had been to buy something promising but relatively modest at the Newmarket sales. His first sight of Delgany Girl in Ireland enlarged his ideas and fired his ambitions.

Her owner was a happily inefficient chancer named Ryan, whom Bastin at once took to when they met at the veterinary conference. They drank endless pints of stout together. Ryan, dispensing pound notes as if he were seeding a new lawn, said jovially that he was about to go broke. He would have to sell his stables in County Meath. This was a pity, because along with the premises would have to go this filly of his, who had the makings of a winner all the way. She was a beauty. Why didn't Bastin come to the country at the weekend and take a look at her?

Bastin did. What started as a casually entered-into engagement to have a few more pints in fresh surroundings after an inspection of a young horse commended by a man whose opinions he respected, ended with the temporary financial rescue of Ryan by Bastin's purchase of a one-third share in Delgany Girl. She was everything that Ryan had said she was. Bastin's share in her cost all of his available capital.

After that things became rather complicated.

The contract agreed to and signed by Bastin and Ryan was an intricate one. In addition to Bastin's one-third share there was an option clause. Bastin had the right, if he chose to exercise it, to make an outright purchase of the mare within a period of two months following her third birthday, at a price to be decided as equitable by a mutually agreed firm of reputable auctioneers in Dublin.

The valuation would clearly depend upon how well Delgany Girl ran before the option date. She ran brilliantly well. She won almost everything that she was entered for. By the time that Ryan reluctantly offered formally to honour his side of the bargain, the value put upon the mare by the auctioneers was £10,000 more than Bastin could afford.

Bastin was by now obsessed with her. His bank manager laughed cynically when he tried to raise a loan on the security of a horse, to be repaid from betting and stake money. Bastin knew of no other sources likely to provide personal finance. The notion of forming a syndicate arrived in his mind one morning while he was having a bath.

The more he thought about it, the more he liked it. It would, he decided early on in his thinking, have to be a military syndicate. This had nothing to do with a sentimental devotion to the army. Its rationale was that it was within the commissioned ranks of the army that he was known and trusted as a judge without equal of which horses moved fast, and lasted, and in what conditions. Complementary to the exploitation of his reputation was the consideration that it was with his professional admirers that the money lay. A fairly accurate rule of thumb was that the military rich congregated in regiments in which the horse held sway.

Bastin, after a round of individual presentations of his flotation to a clientele selected by him for their known interests, expertise, and fat bank balances, had no difficulty whatsoever in securing firm offers for sixteen shares at £500 a go.

The remaining £2000 remained tantalizingly out of reach. Some conditional bids were withdrawn for private reasons unconcerned with lack of confidence in the enterprise. One guaranteed subscriber was killed in a hunting accident. Another certainty was out of touch, shooting big game in East Africa. The time limit of two months from Delgany Girl's third birthday was approaching dangerously fast.

It was at this time that Molly Bastin, a young woman with a business brain that rivalled her sensational construction, suggested that the outstanding four shares should be hawked about to sub-syndicates. The less well-heeled officers serving in line regiments and supporting arms could hardly be expected to find £500 apiece even for an investment as attractive as was Delgany Girl, said Molly, a practising sociologist before the term had been invented. Why not offer them the chance to contribute to a kitty, or rather four kitties? They could do their own organizing. So long as one nominee came forward with £500 to be registered in his own name, Bastin had no need to bother about where the money came from or how the profits were later distributed. The market was there for the tapping. Molly herself would do some of the salesmanship if Bastin thought that that would help.

Bastin hugged her gratefully. Contrived exposure at the right time of the more usually hidden bits of Molly had clinched many a Bastin deal in the past. Molly went to work.

Sub-syndicates from Aldershot Command, Northern Command and Salisbury Plain paid up smartly within a week of slightly scandalous promotional tours by Molly. London District, her fourth and last target, was a harder nut to crack, and indeed was found to be uncrackable unless Molly extended her trawl to sources beyond those initially regarded as acceptable.

There were too many Guardees who looked with distaste at what to their fastidious minds was clearly akin to playing housey-housey with Other Ranks in the NAAFI. There was a freak preponderance of officers in less exclusive organizations strapped by school fees and household bills. Two likely marks showed tentative willing, but confessed belatedly and surprisingly to partnership with dominant wives consumed by evangelical religious fervour who viewed anything to do with the turf as sinful.

Matters were becoming critical. There were six days left in which to pay Ryan and acquire Delgany Girl. Molly's collaborator in the London district sub-syndicate, a Sapper captain who would become its nominee if enough capital were ever assembled to qualify him for nomination, ticked off the last name on his list.

'Four hundred quid spoken for,' he said disgustedly. 'One hundred to go, and no one left to get it from except the cadets at the Shop. Not a hope. We'll have to abandon it.'

Molly, a never-say-die girl, seized upon the Sapper's reference to what was not a hope. Her social science researches had not so far embraced the Shop.

'What cadets? What Shop?' asked Molly.

The Sapper explained about why aspirant officers of the Royal Engineers and the Royal Artillery were trained at the Shop, the Royal Military Academy at Woolwich instead of at the Royal Military College at Sandhurst. Any fool could get into Sandhurst, he said with the prejudiced certainty of a product of the Shop. You needed brains to get into the RMA. Of relevance to the subject under discussion was that unlike Sandhurst, where there was a thick dilution of wealthy half-wits, destined for bodies like the Brigade of Guards and the cavalry, the cadets at the Shop came from middle-class families, lived on minuscule allowances from home, and were perpetually stony broke. The question of the distribution of brainpower in relation to inherited wealth was of considerable genetic interest and if Molly would like . . .

Molly interrupted him.

'What sort of brainpower? At this Shop place I mean. Mathematical?'

'Yes. And Engineering and so on.'

'Well, if they understand even elementary arithmetic they'll recognize a good thing when it's shown to 'em. Do you know anyone there?'

'Yes. My young brother Nigel. He's one of the under-officers.'

'How much can he afford?'

'Nothing.'

Molly did a quick sum.

'Look,' she said, 'at a pinch he could raise four quid? He and twenty-four others. That's your hundred for you. Tell 'em they can't lose.'

'Better if you told them. You'd be more persuasive. Besides, there's a point of discipline and proper conduct. It would be quite wrong for me to use my rank to try to induce young cadets to put up money that they can't afford to invest in a speculative . . .'

Molly stared grimly at this toffee-nosed Pom who seemed intent upon throwing a fortune away.

'OK,' she said, 'you're on. You get your kid brother to line up the starters. I'll give them the works.'

She did it convincingly in a private room in a pub in Gravesend. They drooled at her while she spoke earnestly of the characteristics of the mare, and gave a businesslike rundown of its prospects. Periodically she adjusted the hem of her skirt absent-mindedly, heaved her bosom about, and poked the end of her pink tongue between her teeth. Not only would they get a negotiable share in a wonder horse, she told them, with a steady return from its prize money, but the syndicate would also furnish its members with confidential inside information on Delgany Girl's current form before every race and would advise on ante-post betting. It was a snip, she concluded simply, taking a deep breath and holding it.

The consequences of the deep breath did the trick of converting the last waverers. During the next few days bank managers, fathers, uncles, usurers, moneyed friends and one pawnbroker, were badgered for advances. The collective shirt of twenty-five Woolwich cadets was handed over in notes to the Sapper captain by his younger brother Nigel ('A sweet boy,' as Molly said). The Sapper gave it to Molly, who gave it to Bastin, who paid it into his bank, which wrote out a certified cheque to Ryan two days before the expiry of the deadline.

Delgany Girl, who would still be trained by Ryan, became the joint property of Bastin and the syndicate. Ryan acknowledged the accretion to his finances with pleasure, felt desperately sentimental about the deletion of his name from the part ownership of a horse that he loved, and became and stayed constructively drunk. This led to flaws in the paperwork.

At Leopardstown, in her first race in her new colours, Delgany Girl came in first by two lengths at two to one. The stake was modest, and went to pay partially for Bastin's legitimate expenses in setting up the syndicate.

In succession Delgany Girl was second at Navan and won again at Limerick Junction. Bastin's expenses were paid in full. From her next victory and thereafter, Delgany Girl would bring comfort and profit to all the shareholders, large and small, who owned her.

Bastin telephoned the good news to most of them. Molly made it her personal business to tell the Sapper captain, who relayed it to his brother. There was rejoicing in destitute cadet circles at the Shop.

Delgany Girl's next scheduled race was in England, at Catterick Bridge. She was the odds-on favourite ante post, and the stake money was the highest among her four entries under the new proprietorship. She became half crazed with fright during a wild sea crossing from Dunlaoghaire, was soothed by her groom, and appeared to have recovered her equanimity by the time she came ashore at Holyhead. It was an illusory calmness. She bolted from the jetty. She galloped in a frenzy along the railway line, fell and broke a leg. She had to be destroyed.

Bastin, Molly and Ryan, all of whom genuinely loved the mare as a mare, were thrown into a deep grief. They were pulled out of it by the urgent need to deal with a new and daunting crisis, arising from a muddle. Ryan's post-sale interlude of dogged consolation from the bottle had combined with Bastin's single-minded euphoria over the successful conclusion of the deal to cause an oversight.

Ryan, in a confused morning at his desk on the day after the

61

sale, had found that his insurance policy was due for renewal. He had given a blurred look to what he was insuring, had removed Delgany Girl from the list on the reasonable grounds that she was no longer his, and had reduced the size of his premium cheque proportionately. All this was defensible, or would have been if he had first cleared it with Bastin. Ryan had meant to, but had forgotten. He had forgotten quite a few other things at the time.

Bastin, who should have checked carefully that everything was in sound order, had simply assumed that Ryan, who was still training Delgany Girl, would continue to insure her and would include the cost of the premium in the quarterly bills that he submitted.

The Bastin–Ryan dispute, although prolonged, interesting and heavy with acrimony, was of academic significance to the members of the syndicate. What mattered to them was that their asset was both dead and uninsured. All investments were a total loss.

Bastin went back to living on his major's pay and wrangled with Ryan, who was incapable of paying anybody anything, through solicitors. The sixteen £500 shareholders shrugged off their losses with the embittered philosophical resignation of the rich. A certain amount of domestic merry hell broke out in the households of representative members of the Aldershot Command, Northern Command and Salisbury Plain syndicates, and in those of four-fifths of the membership of the London District syndicate. Among the small-timers who held the residual equity of one-fifth of the London District stock, the twenty-five Woolwich cadets, there was consternation, fury, loud calls for restitution and gloomy pondering upon the realities of long stretches of penury.

This unrest crystallized into action of a sort at a mass indignation meeting. The Sapper captain's under-officer brother, Molly's sweet boy Nigel, was given a mandate, defined in the vernacular, to take whatever steps he thought fit to recover with the least delay the four pounds a head that the shareholders had been lured into contributing. (The actual wording was: 'Tell that thieving bastard of a brother of yours, and that sexpot with the tits, that unless they get someone to pay up we'll bloody flay them alive.')

Nigel summarized this message orally to his brother. After a blistering ten minutes, the Sapper captain concluded that his safest way out was to pass the buck to Molly. He telephoned and outlined the situation. He did not get the rebuff that he had expected. She listened with sympathetic attention.

'Send that sweet boy to me,' she said throatily at last, 'I'll see what I can do for him.'

Nigel borrowed the fare from his brother and caught the next train to Aldershot.

Molly was waiting for him in the sitting room of a house in a row of officers' quarters. Although it was early in the afternoon the curtains were drawn. Two table lamps gave a subdued, diffused light. Molly, wearing a low-cut summer dress, shook hands courteously with him, ushered him to an armchair on one side of the fireplace, and herself sat opposite him in another. He noticed that she wasn't all that efficient at sitting in armchairs. Every time she shifted her weight her skirt climbed a little further above her knees.

As she began to speak he stared, transfixed alternately by what he could see of her top-hamper and by what he could see of her undercarriage. (At that early stage of his military career he kept mixing his interservice metaphors. Years later he did well in Combined Operations.) Molly talked easily, still using the husky voice that she had used on the telephone to his brother. It was inconsequential chatter, broken by pauses for viewing. When she calculated that Nigel had seen enough for his own good, she gently led him to the business of the day.

'Tell me, Nigel,' she said softly, 'all about it.'

Nigel, whose resolution had been crumbling catastrophically, wrenched his mind back to the purpose of his visit. He did it impressively. He made no attempt to evade his own responsibility for the fiasco. Influenced by his brother and by Molly, he said, but entirely convinced by what they had told him, he had persuaded twenty-four of his fellow cadets to invest money that they could not afford in a get-rich-quick scheme that had failed. For himself, he had learned his lesson.

But that was only part of it. The hardships didn't end at him. And, frankly, it was because of her that his friends were in debt. Four pounds a head mightn't seem much to her, but he could assure her that in 1925 it meant an awful lot to a Woolwich cadet.

She wriggled in her chair again. He looked down, blushed, looked up fast, manfully kept his eyes moving upwards across her bosom, until they met *her* eyes. He suddenly felt greatly moved. Two big tears had formed. They rolled slowly down her convex cheeks.

He couldn't go on with what he had meant to say. Instead he cleared his throat and said, 'That's all.'

Molly held his gaze, for a long time. She blinked repeatedly. She dried her eyes on a lace-edged handkerchief. Then she rose sinuously to her feet, walked to a writing desk and opened a drawer. He heard her scrabbling about inside. Her back masked what she was doing, but he heard the scratch of a pen. When she turned around she was sealing an envelope, licking the gum on the flap with that enticing pink tongue of hers. There were tears in her eyes again.

'I'm going to make you a little speech, Nigel,' she said gently. 'To be honest, when I suggested to your brother that you should come and see me, I didn't know what I was going to say to you. My husband and I have been harder hit financially by this business than anyone else. I thought that what I'd do was hear you out, and then tell you as kindly as I could that I was unable to help, however sympathetic I was. But when you . . . but when you . . .'

Her voice broke. She recovered herself, smiled through a renewed fall of tears, and carried on.

'But when you spoke of the trouble you were in, and then when you refused to make a meal of it and just said, "That's all," then . . . then I was so touched that I just had to do something for you. I don't care what I have to sacrifice to compensate for it. So please . . . please give my apologies, and love, to all those other lovely cadets, and take this.'

She finished in a rush. She handed over the envelope.

'You have your money back,' she said simply. She dried her

eyes again. The envelope was bulky to his touch. He stared at her wordlessly, delightedly. She sealed the delight by stepping towards him, lacing her hands behind his neck, squeezing, and giving him a smacking kiss. When she disengaged she walked to the front door and opened it.

'Now go, sweet boy,' she said.

He turned once as he walked down the road, feeling as happy as he had ever felt in his life. She was still standing in her doorway. She blew him a kiss, and waved. He waved back.

He was halfway to Waterloo in the train before his mental and emotional stability was fully restored. He opened the envelope. There were four one pound notes in it, wrapped in eight sheets of blank writing paper.

SARCASM AT BLANKIPUR.

Cavalry Instructor (to Mounted Infantry Man). 'ULLO! I THOUGHT IT WAS YOU THAT WROTE HOME LAST MAIL – 'MOTHER, YOU SHOULD SEE ME RIDE!'

SHORT ORDER

THE directing staff on the Platoon Commanders'
Course were ardent and dedicated young men,
commissioned from Sandhurst in the late 1930s,
selected as instructors for their skills and qualities, precluded
frustratingly by those qualities from serving as they had hoped
with the British Expeditionary Force in France and Belgium
in 1939 and 1940. Submissions by them to join the BEF had
been refused with curtness. They were reminded that they had
a job to do, training. They were among the few available with
the knowledge and ability to do it. Their duty was to do it.

They did it dutifully, with an enhanced intensity of purpose
after the defeat of the French and Belgian armies and the
evacuation of the bulk of the BEF from Dunkirk. Britain was in
danger of invasion. There was an electric air of urgency about
the conduct of the Platoon Commanders' Course.

Problems for students, most of them not much younger than
the directing staff, were set. Responses were considered and
criticized. The staff solution to each problem, not the *only*
solution it was stressed, but a workable solution, was put
forward for discussion and analysis. New ideas were sought,
and were praised or discarded.

One of the standard problems was to do with the capture of
a bridge. It was a small, rural bridge that spanned a small,
rural river. Beyond the bridge were a complex of farm
buildings and a copse, both theoretically occupied by the
enemy. Students were taken in groups of five to view the
ground. They were given five minutes to do so. Then they were
sent away to think about it. Come back in half an hour, they

were told, and give your orders for a platoon attack.

Among one of the groups of five was an unusual subaltern, much older than his fellow students, much older than the directing staff. He wore on his battledress blouse the ribbon of the Military Cross and the ribbons of the war medal and the victory medal, Mutt and Jeff of the First World War. He was a bald, sturdy man of few words, who had volunteered again in 1939.

His contemplation of the bridge was cursory. The directing staff noted with disapproval that during the half-hour allowed for consideration his mind seemed not to be on his work. He smoked two cigarettes, and became absorbed in watching birds.

The students reassembled. One by one they issued their orders. The first four were competently delivered, well-thought-out offerings given in the approved sequence: Information, Intention, Method, Inter-Communication, Administration. The generally favoured line was of a noisy feint attack from the front, backed by extensive use of smoke from the two-inch mortar, while the real assaulting party forded the river upstream, made their way unseen to the farm and the copse, and took the position from the rear.

The directing staff nodded in endorsement, promoted argument on points of detail, and marked ticks against names on the lists on their clipboards.

The bald old-timer was last. His orders were succinct. He drew his pistol, waved it above his head, and shouted: 'CHARGE!'

The directing staff were appalled. They explained coldly why they were appalled. The whole purpose of the course, they said, was to instil into the minds of junior officers the need for subtlety, careful planning, rigorous control and exact timing.

The bald subaltern was unrepentant. He looked mildly puzzled. 'Well, that's what I did last time I took a bridge,' he said reminiscently, 'And what's more they gave me the MC for it.'

TO STRETCH A POINT

H ARRIS, the manager of a not very productive farm in Tanganyika, suffered a mild attack of patriotism in 1938 when Germany invaded Czechoslovakia. Harris volunteered for the reserve of the King's African Rifles.

It was an undemanding organization, short of warlike paraphernalia. The one regular officer, seconded as the adjutant, operated upon a basis of training pamphlets and improvisation. Harris and his friends were instructed in elementary drill, fired a few weapons, and were introduced to TEWTs – tactical exercises without troops. There weren't many troops. Tanganyika was one of the poorer colonies. The administration couldn't afford the expense.

When war was declared in 1939, Harris was surprised, gratified and embarrassed to find that overnight he had become a company commander. He doubted the wisdom of this appointment and told the adjutant so. He didn't know enough, said Harris. The adjutant told him curtly and unflatteringly that there wasn't anybody else. If Harris was bothered by military ignorance he would simply have to read the pamphlets and take it from there. The outbreak of war had loosened the government's purse strings, and recruits were coming in in large numbers. Harris's job was to train, equip, administer, discipline and lead these people, and he'd better get on with it.

Harris got on with it. He found himself enjoying it. His new soldiers took their task seriously, and he slowly moulded them into the semblance of an infantry company. He had little to guide him but the pamphlets. The battalion was dispersed over a wide area, and the recently arrived colonel and his adjutant were as often as not dealing with problems elsewhere.

In his few unoccupied moments Harris pondered on the unreality of what he was doing. This was precautionary soldiering, supervised by an amateur, him, rehearsing Africans in defensive preparations against an imaginary threat. No conceivable enemy would try to attack Tanganyika.

.But the prospect became more real when Italy entered the war in the summer of 1940. Harris's battalion was included in the Force that invaded Italian Somaliland.

With action imminent, Harris took a further look at the pamphlet that listed the details of a company's establishment. He had got most of it right, with a correct distribution of NCOs, riflemen, Lewis gunners, the signaller, the runner and so on, but he was annoyed at one omission. He had forgotten to nominate the two necessary stretcher-bearers.

He appointed them on the following morning. On the day after that the two deserted. The company sergeant-major, Harris's guru on all matters to do with African custom and religion, explained why, with tact. These men were warriors, he said. They had enlisted to fight. Tending wounded wasn't fighting. The two deserters had been beset by shame. Anyone who returned to his village after the war and said that he had been a stretcher-bearer would become a laughing-stock, scorned by the women.

Harris said that that was all very well, and that he now understood the difficulty, but he still had to have stretcher-bearers. Aside from the fact that the pamphlet said that he should, they would obviously be useful. What did the sergeant-major suggest?

The sergeant-major suggested a rotational system: two men ordered to do an unpopular job for not more than a week at a time, on the understanding that when their stint was up they would get back to real men's work. The sharing of the load should minimize complaints.

Harris sensibly took this advice.

Some months later, amidst very hot rocks on a very hot day in

Somalia, Harris led a bayonet charge against an Italian position. It was rather less dangerous than the term suggests. The attackers were debilitated by thirst, and the defenders were affected by a mixture of lethargy and lack of interest in the profession to which they had been conscripted. None the less Harris, feeling slightly foolish, did his best to inject some authenticity into the proceedings. He drew his pistol, and shouted. 'Fix bayonets,' and led from the front. He was pleased to find that his parched followers began to show signs of increased enthusiasm as they neared the objective. He was less pleased to notice that the most excited of the lot was one of that week's stretcher-bearers.

According to Harris's lodestar, the pamphlet, the stretcher-bearers should have been trotting discreetly in the wake of the assault, ready to succour stricken comrades. This particular stretcher-bearer was exceeding his instructions. The stretcher, a clumsy apparatus of thick canvas secured to heavy wooden poles, was still furled by its fastening straps. The bearer was holding it by the handles at one end and was waving it in the air in a state of martial exaltation. Harris saw all this clearly because the stretcher-bearer overtook him in the final run-in.

Most of the Italians came out with their hands up. One, who was slow in doing so, was felled by a fierce crack over the head from the stretcher. He collapsed, unconscious. Harris was starting to wonder what to do next when the stretcher-bearer readjusted his outlook to the requirements of the Geneva Convention. He nodded to his mate and unbuckled the stretcher. Between them they carefully loaded up the victim, the only casualty of the engagement, and carried him to the rear in the way prescribed by Harris and his pamphlets.

BREACH IN A TEACUP

I N the Middle East of the First World War, Colonel
Richard Meinertzhagen, a man of independent means
and of independent mind, demonstrated that he was an
Intelligence operative of notable originality, guile and
dedication. Among his more productive endeavours were a
fruitful collaboration with T.E. Lawrence in the course of the
Arab Revolt, and the authorship and execution of an
ambitiously successful deception plan that badly misled the
Turks whilst General Allenby's army was driving them out of
Palestine. Colonel Meinertzhagen was as touchy and short-
tempered in his dealings with his colleagues, superiors and
subordinates as he was astute in the exercise of his professional
talents.

In 1940, in common with large numbers of his generation,
the by now retired colonel answered the call for volunteers to
enlist in the Home Guard. This body was formed hastily to
help to defend Britain against what looked like imminent
German invasion. Private Meinertzhagen's unit operated in
the West End of London, where most of its members lived.

He was on duty one night in December 1940 when his
platoon was visited by a government minister, keen to do his
duty to keep up the spirits of the people. The German invasion
had yet to materialize, but officially the threat still existed.
The Blitz was well under way, and bombs fell nightly on
London. The platoon, who could afford that sort of thing,
invited the minister to dinner.

The minister became expansive after dinner. He gave a
short and stimulating address. It may seem to his hearers, he

said confidentially, that British arms abroad were discouragingly inactive at the moment. But believe you him, and mark his words, he knew. A British offensive in the Western Desert was in the advanced stages of planning and would shortly be mounted against the Italian armies on the Egyptian–Libyan frontier. British tails would soon be well and truly up. Et cetera.

Meinertzhagen, the former Intelligence specialist, was appalled by this cavalier indifference by a politician to the requirements of military security. He considered that it could only be contained by representations to as close to the top as he could get. A fuss raised by him lower down the scale would only stimulate additional damaging talk. Meinertzhagen asked for an urgent and private appointment with a general with whom he had once served, now the Director of Military Operations at the War Office.

The DMO was even more appalled than was Meinertzhagen. A large Italian army had been edging ponderously from Libya over the Egyptian border almost from the time that Italy had entered the war in the previous June. The Italians were ill trained, ill directed and ineptly disposed. Plans to attack and destroy them were near full maturity.

Preparations had been conducted with exemplary secrecy. In the Middle East only General Wavell, the Commander-in-Chief, and General O'Connor, who was to lead the attacking force, knew of what was afoot. Subordinate commanders and their formations had been exercised in movement and conditions similar to those that would prevail in the forthcoming fighting, but had been led to believe that the exercises were just an advanced form of routine training. In Britain, knowledge of the impending attack was confined to the Prime Minister, the Secretary of State for War, the Chief of the Imperial General Staff and the DMO himself. These made a total of six people, in both Cairo and London, in the know.

The errant minister was at once interrogated. He had had no access to a leak of inside information, he said. He had simply drawn his own conclusions from what he had heard on the wireless and had read in the newspapers. From these open sources he had worked out where the British were now best placed to attack an enemy. The Middle East was the only obvious starter. Given a national leader of the belligerence of Mr Winston Churchill it was clear that no opportunity for offensive action would be allowed to pass unexploited. The minister had said what he had said to his Home Guard audience partly because he had believed that it must be true, but mostly with the rather simple-minded intention of raising morale and of cheering everybody up.

The minister, loaded with reproach and stricken with remorse, went away determined to be more sensible in future. General O'Connor's attack went in on time, was developed brilliantly, and destroyed or captured almost all of the Italian army in Cyrenaica plus most of its impedimenta. And Field Marshal Lord Cavan sent for Meinertzhagen.

Lord Cavan was a prickly Guardee who believed that things should be done in the right way. He had been a corps commander of note during the First World War, and he now commanded the London area of the Home Guard. It had come to his notice, he said, that Meinertzhagen had been seen paying a call upon a senior officer in the War Office. Before taking this step had Meinertzhagen first sought the approval of his commanding officer?

Meinertzhagen said No, he hadn't. The matter had been urgent, and of high security significance. There had been no time to discuss it with his commanding officer even if he had wanted to, which he hadn't. It had been far too delicate for bandying about at that sort of low level.

Lord Cavan was unused to hearing private soldiers describing their colonels to him as being of a low level. He said so. He added a great deal more. Meinertzhagen's statement, he said, was disgraceful. So was his attitude. Meinertzhagen must get it into his head once and for all that the Home Guard might seem to some to be an amateurish organization, but it was an embodied part of His Majesty's forces. He, Cavan, was responsible for the performance and discipline of his component of it. The disciplinary standards that he set for it were precisely those of the regular army. It would degenerate into an uncontrolled rabble if those members of the rank and file who had friends in high places were to be allowed to go over the heads of their superiors to raise matters of military importance about which those superiors should properly be informed or consulted.

The temperature of the interview, already several degrees above normal, reached new heights when Meinertzhagen said that so far as the case at issue was concerned Lord Cavan was talking nonsense. The intregrity of a military secret, or of any other secret for that matter, diminished in direct proportion to the number of people who shared it. It would have been an act of unpatriotic idiocy to confide it to his commanding officer.

Lord Cavan said that Meinhertzhagen was sacked.

Until this point the encounter was no more than a fierce disagreement between two angry old men, each convinced that he was right. Meinertzhagen raised it to a new, inspired level.

'I will not be spoken to like that by an Irish Field Marshal,' he said, in a mixture of *hauteur*, insubordination, originality, racism and irrelevance, of great appeal to those of us who only think of what we could have said, if only we'd thought of it, about ten minutes after the person we've been arguing with has gone away.*

Meinertzhagen departed in rage and triumph and got into a taxi, which was immediately the victim of a near-miss from a German bomb. Meinertzhagen recovered consciousness in hospital about ten days later. By the time that he was released so much had happened in the Western Desert that ministerial indiscretions and the spirited rows of old soldiers had been forgotten.

---

* Meinertzhagen was in fact on pretty tricky ground. If he'd decided to take on all the Irish Field Marshals of the Second World War and its aftermath he'd have had to confront Alanbrooke, Dill, Alexander, Montgomery, Auchinleck, and Templer – tough going, even for Meinertzhagen.

THE DAPHNE BREAK

WATCHERS of the Fortescues sighed whenever another was born, and did their best, usually unsuccessfully, to keep out of their way when they matured. Fortescue genes travelled in direct succession, and made no concessions to Mendel, Eysenck, the double helix, or anybody or anything else. One Fortescue was a replica of another Fortescue.

Fortescues had good health, good looks, were fearless and vigorous, slow-thinking, and early in life developed an urgent psychological need to immerse themselves self-sacrifically in a cause. This recurrent obsession was accompanied by an inability to focus upon more than one idea at a time and a tendency to press any project that engaged the Fortescue attentions to beyond the bounds of commonsense.

For two and a half centuries the cause that had absorbed a succession of them had been service to the Crown. It hadn't done the Crown much good. Fortescues were prominent in the defeat at Fontenoy, the loss of the American colonies, the destruction at sea of several expensive warships, the Boer victory at Majuba, the failure to rescue General Gordon at Khartoum, and the surrender to the Turks of the besieged garrison of Kut-el-Amara.

Daphne Fortescue, b.1920, demonstrated the family's high-handed way with genetics by exhibiting all the family qualities without the benefit of paternal influence. She was a post-humous baby. Her father, a cavalry officer recruited for hush-hush work in Ireland, had refined his impersonation of a Republican gunman to such a degree of perfection that he was shot dead by a Black and Tan within six days of taking up his duties, an event that generated an embarrassed hullabaloo in Dublin Castle and Whitehall.

He was little missed domestically. Daphne was an obstreperous baby, a wilful and noisy small child, and a relentlessly bossy schoolgirl who shone at games, stood up to mistresses on points of principle and showed a dauntingly precocious enthusiasm for conducting her life as a personal crusade on behalf of truth and righteousness. At that time she had no doubts about the physical location of the bulk of truth and righteousness. She was smack in the middle of it. She was prepared to be tolerant of some foreigners, and to accept that their foreignness was not altogether their fault, but she was not a girl to allow sympathy with an inherent disability to smudge a realistic assessment of deficiencies.

In her first year at Somerville College, Oxford, she passed much time in contemplating how she could best put her talents to use for the good of that part of mankind that was lucky enough to live within the British Empire. She rather thought that she would become a missionary in India.

The outbreak of war in September 1939 changed all that. Here was a worthwhile cause if ever there was one. Daphne at once volunteered for the Auxiliary Territorial Service. She was disappointed to find that there was a surfeit of applicants and an inadequacy of vacancies. Her name was put on a waiting list. In the meanwhile she became a typist at the BBC. It was not the sort of job that provided the complete commitment that she craved, but at least it was war work. During this interlude she became conscientiously proficient with her typewriter, irritated her superiors by the frankness of her advice on how they could improve the running of their departments, and was exposed to what her mother described as *very peculiar influences*. The BBC staff had expanded fast. Some of the new people were almost *socialists*.

Daphne felt ardently self-sacrificial after Dunkirk, followed the daily score in the Battle of Britain closely, and was coolly intrepid throughout the London Blitz. When on leave she bored the pants off her mother by delivering intense and interminable harangues about anti-Fascism on inopportune occasions, such as breakfast. She further discommoded her mother with even richer invective when the BBC exercised its priority right to claim her continuing services when the ATS at last called her up.

Typical blind blimpishness, cried Daphne at her mother. The BBC, the armed forces, the whole conduct of the war, was in the hands of diehard Tory has-beens, living in the past, safeguarding their investments, impervious to the swelling tide of social change that would knock the hell out of outdated shibboleths once the Fascist Beast had been destroyed.

These sentiments upset Daphne's mother on two counts. The first was that she thought it absolutely right that the war should be controlled by Tory diehards, reliable guardians of investments, cherishers of old values, resisters of social change etc. The second was that she was beginning to wonder if those very peculiar influences on her daughter were becoming more influential than was healthy.

On the second one her diagnosis was accurate. Daphne had found a new invigorating cause. It would have had no appeal to earlier Fortescues, but she wrapped herself in it with a similar undiscriminating energy to that shown by her forbears whilst accidentally impeding the march of Empire. She had joined the Communist Party of Great Britain. At much the same time the BBC waived its lien on her employment and she also joined the ATS.

If the ATS had been quicker off the mark in 1939, Daphne would have been a model recruit. By early 1942 she was a military liability. It was some weeks after her enlistment before the extent of the liability was fully appreciated. In one sense she was a credit to her uniform. She was clean, smart, well turned-out, kept her back hair clear of her collar, shone her shoes and her brasses and seemed to take pleasure in drill. She was meticulous about addressing sergeants as sergeant and officers as ma'am, and she threw up an elegant salute. It was when she opened her mouth that misgivings accumulated. She opened it with progressive frequency.

'It must be encouraging, ma'am, for our Russian allies,' she would say deadpan, 'while they're fighting for their lives at the gates of Moscow, to know that barrackroom 6B in this place has been cleaned to a state of perfection.'

Or: 'Do you perhaps think, sergeant, that that 3-tonner that's taking the off-duty girls into Chester for the dance might be better used by the Red Army at Smolensk?'

Or: 'It's amazing, really, that the countryside around here is swarming with troops playing silly games on exercises while their Russian comrades are bleeding to death.'

These commentaries were always put forward with a scrupulous, grim courtesy. They attracted no disciplinary action, only some off-the-record criticism: 'That girl Fortescue is a bit Bolshie, ma'am,' said Daphne's sergeant. What did stimulate disciplinary reprisal was the hereditary single-mindedness with which Daphne moved to the next logical step in support of her newly acquired creed. She daubed the outer walls of the orderly room with large-lettered slogans in red paint, advocating SECOND FRONT NOW. She followed this up by addressing an impromptu meeting in the NAAFI canteen on the subject of a criminal crypto-fascist capitalist conspiracy led by the jackal Churchill, and aimed at the reduction of Russia to rubble and of the Russians to ashes by Churchill's secret ally, Hitler, prior to a share-out of the territorial plunder between the predators.

She was arrested, diffidently, by a lance corporal of the military police, who had been invited in for a cup of tea by his ATS girlfriend and who hadn't expected to find himself having to deal with a stridently articulate female orator promoting what he supposed must be treason or suchlike. She went with him quietly and with dignity. There was no precedent for the arrest of an ATS girl, and no prepared accommodation for locking one up. After much genteel cursing and hand-wringing by ma'am, and prolonged persuasion of a reluctant medical officer, Daphne was put into a room in the sick quarters. She was guarded by relays of ATS Other Ranks, working in pairs. Most resented the task. Some thought it a bit of a lark.

During the next few days, while Daphne stayed in what, she

admitted to herself, was a rather comfortable form of confinement, there was a great deal of telephoning between ma'am, district headquarters, the judge advocate general's department and a junior minister in the War Office. All of them advanced conflicting arguments about the military and political drawbacks to a public trial of Daphne, and all of them accepted sorrowfully that they could think of no means of avoiding one.

Daphne solved their problem for them. She escaped from custody. It was no blind, instinctive flight from judicial retribution. It was an imaginatively planned excursion, and its ultimate destination was Russia. There, Daphne knew, she could offer her services to the Red Army, in which women fought alongside men in proletarian solidarity. It was an exhilarating prospect.

The agent who brought this journey within the bounds of possibility was a girl named Denise, a compact, world-weary-looking brunette from Liverpool whom Daphne had noticed showing signs of muted appreciation during the canteen speech. Daphne had never before spoken to her, but did so at length, repeatedly, when Denise turned up as a regular member of the night shift of Daphne's guards. Denise was contemptuous of her orders. She brought in mugs of tea and chatted to Daphne.

After some preliminary verbal fencing, Denise revealed that she too was a Party member, of some years' standing. She belonged to a small cell on Merseyside. The cell, she said rather wistfully, operated under strict Party discipline in conditions of rigorous security, and she much admired the freedom that had been bestowed upon Daphne to speak her mind openly and with such effect. Until she had joined the ATS, Denise's role had been less glamorous and more exacting. Her cell had assembled information about shipping coming in and out of Liverpool. Denise's contribution had been to pick up seamen, sleep with them, and pry Intelligence from them. She wasn't by nature promiscuous or anything like that, mind, but everyone had to make *some* sacrifices in the interests of the Party.

Daphne said that she admired that sort of dedication. Denise asked how far Daphne would be prepared to go to serve the Party. Daphne said that she put no bounds on it. She knew that it was an impossible dream, but her one, burning ambition was to take up arms and *fight* in the ranks of her Russian comrades. Denise made no immediate comment, but a seed was sown. On her next forty-eight-hour pass to Liverpool she took measures to advance its germination.

The scheme, when its details had been tied up, was of almost childish simplicity. A member of Denise's cell was a merchant seaman. It was not yet public knowledge, but British convoys, escorted by the Royal Navy, were making increasingly frequent trips to deliver war material to the Russian Arctic port of Murmansk. The seaman was due to go on the next one. He had total confidence in his ability to smuggle a stowaway aboard his ship and to keep her hidden. All that Daphne would have to do was to break out of her unbarred prison room, hitch-hike to Liverpool, contact the sailor at a designated pub at a designated time and leave the mechanics of embarkation to him. She would need civilian clothes for the road journey; Denise would fix those. A sweater and slacks would suffice. Any questions?

Daphne, enchanted and delighted, had none. She could only say, she said, thank you. Denise then looked mildly hesitant, but not too hesitant. 'You did say,' she said firmly, 'that there were no bounds to what you would do to help the Party. No bounds were your words.'

'Yes,' said Daphne.

'Like I put no bounds on how *I* served the Party.'

'Yes,' said Daphne.

'Well,' said Denise, 'it might turn out to be something rather like that. There are three Party members in the crew. It's a long, rough trip. They're used to sharing everything in the Party. They've not often had a woman aboard before. They're men, and I know men, and I don't know how well you know men, but I think you can take it for granted that from time to time, well . . .'

'I understand,' said Daphne bravely.

Daphne, feeling resolute and adventurous, climbed out of the window of the sick quarters in the small hours of a moonlit night, while Denise did the not very difficult job of diverting the attentions of her fellow guard. Daphne carried the sweater and slacks in a carrier bag brought to her by Denise. The camp was silent. The sentries were somnolent. The way out was by a popular route under the strands of perimeter wire, much used by girls who saw no reason to let the requirements of good order and military discipline interfere with their love lives. Within twenty minutes of leaving her room, Daphne had changed into the surface civilian clothes, hidden her uniform tunic and skirt in the undergrowth of a copse, and was walking briskly along the Chester road. Shortly after dawn a doctor on his way to an urgent sick call gave her a lift almost into Chester. She caught an early bus into Liverpool. She was there by ten o'clock.

Promptly at noon she made her way to the designated pub in Broad Street. She had been told to sit at a corner table, and to keep an eye open for a dark-haired thirtyish sailor in a donkey jacket who answered to the name of Frank. Denise, admirably professional, had carefully rehearsed her in identification procedures. Frank would say, 'Have you heard from Dixie Dean lately?' The authorized reply was, 'No, but I think he's with Uncle Joe.'

She spotted Frank at once. He was drinking a pint of mild at the bar, and he was clearly a professional too. He looked unobtrusively around, let his gaze fall on her without recognition, slowly finished his pint and then drifted quietly towards her. He spoke his piece about Dixie Dean from the corner of his mouth. She gave the Uncle Joe formula in a low clear voice. He nodded at the door, and walked out. She followed.

'The essence of good planning is to keep it simple,' said Frank. Pete and Jacko, also in donkey jackets, also thirtyish, nodded. They hadn't said much since Frank had introduced them to Daphne in the drinking club to which he had led her. She had taken rather a liking to Frank. She was less sure of these two.

Then she had brought herself to order. Likes and dislikes, emotions of any kind were irrelevant, despicable. The cause was higher than the individual. These were comrades in a great movement. She wished all the same that Jacko would do something about that furtive leer of his, but . . .

'The simplest way to get a seaman aboard a ship without too many questions being asked is to carry him up the gangway dead drunk,' said Frank.

'You want me to pretend to be drunk?' asked Daphne, smiling. She was taken with the idea. Amateur theatricals were one of her loves.

'Not pretend to be drunk,' said Frank, not smiling. '*Be* drunk. I'm taking no chances. It's got to be one hundred per cent authentic. We'll tank you up with the hard stuff, put you in a duffle coat and a woollen cap over your hair, wrap a scarf around your face and carry you aboard. Out cold.'

Pete and Jacko nodded again. Daphne thought hard, shuddered a little, recognized another touch of complete professionalism and looked determined. 'Right, boys,' she said resolutely, 'tank me up.'

She remembered nothing after the fifth rum and chaser. She awoke, feeling terrible, on a dingy bunk in a boxlike small steel room with blistered, stained paint on its walls. There was an overhead light, and a distant throbbing, less intrusive than the closer throbbing of her head. The floor tilted one way, and then back again, in a slow rhythm.

She sat up shakily, and saw with disgust that she had been sick over the duffle coat that she was wearing. She stumbled to the door. It was locked. She noticed a smaller door, behind which she found a lavatory and a tiny wash-basin. She freshened herself up. There was no towel, but she dried herself on her sweater. She felt slightly, very slightly, better.

Half an hour later she felt infinitely better, after a moment of alarm when she heard a key turning in the lock and saw the door open.

It was Frank. He carried two brown paper bags. In one was a packet of corned beef sandwiches and a corked half whisky bottle of rapidly cooling tea. In the other, larger one, were a few toilet things, a man's shirt, two pairs of heavy woollen socks and a set of Long John combination underwear. 'Not much,' said Frank, 'but the best we can do. There won't be much variety in the grub either. But it'll keep you going. It's only for two weeks or so. We're already at sea. We'll probably have to hang about a bit while the convoy forms up in the Clyde, but then it'll be a straight run.'

Daphne felt a sudden, huge elation. Her hangover seemed to fly away. 'Thank you, Frank,' she said intently.

Frank looked her carefully up and down. 'You can thank me properly later,' he said, with meaning.

There were no portholes in the little cabin, and Daphne had no watch. She was unable to distinguish night from day. The only indication of the passage of time came from the periodic delivery, usually by Frank, sometimes by Pete or Jacko, of her food. There was plenty of it, but it was always the same. Corned beef sandwiches, tepid tea.

On the second day, as she munched her sandwiches, Frank explained to her about the cabin. The ship was a freighter, and before the war had also carried a small number of passengers. The passenger accommodation had since been broken down to make more room for cargo, but Daphne's little cabin, once lived in by a nurse who was available to the passengers, was too small, and too inconveniently placed, to be worth modifying. It had been left as it was, deep in the bowels of the ship, no view from a porthole, aired by a creaking ventilation shaft, a memorial to the greed of the capitalist system that lodged its employees economically in squalor while the fat-cat fare-paying passengers frolicked in luxury above. It was ironic, said Frank, staring at her, that this relic of capitalist exploitation was now being put to use to take to the motherland of the Revolution a convert to the cause with an understanding of her responsibilities as well as of her privileges.

He continued to stare at her. She stared back. This was it. The time had come to thank Frank, practically. She thanked Frank. An adaptation of some traditional advice once given to her by her mother helped her. Daphne lay back, closed her eyes and thought of the Comintern.

After that, she found herself thanking Frank with frequency. She felt faintly mutinous when it became necessary to thank Pete and Jacko too, but they were less regular deliverers of her sandwiches and tea, and she fought down her distaste with the aid of some self-mockery about how difficult she found it to shed the outmoded concepts of bourgeois morality that had been instilled into her. Strengthened by these thoughts, and with her eyes shut once more, she demonstrated her gratitude. It was a consoling thought that although she had no track of time by conventional means, a lot of it had passed. She could judge that by the number of corned beef sandwiches that she had eaten. the total, at three helpings a day, was entering the fifties.

None the less she was surprised, and became nearly transported with joy, when one night, or day, or whenever it was, Frank told her that they were nearing their destination. He wanted to brief her about the manner of her disembark-ation, he said. She was to pay very close attention. She did.

'You'll have to get off by yourself,' he said. 'If you go to our Russian friends with me or Pete or Jacko in tow, our cover will be blown to the captain. He's supposed to be an ally of the Russians, just like everyone else is *supposed* to be, but like most of them he's just another capitalist, plutocrat's lackey. I can't risk the breaking up of the cell. So this is what you'll do. When we tie up in Murmansk everyone except the duty watch will go ashore. Just before we go I'll unlock your door. You wait half an hour – you'll have to guess it – and then go out. There's a complicated layout of ladders and things, but just pick any of 'em and keep climbing. You'll come to the deck where the gangway is. There'll be someone manning the top of it, but he won't pay any attention to you. He'll probably take you for a Russian woman official. Lots of them about. Then all you do is walk down the gangway. The bottom of it's in a huge sort of shed. Do you speak Russian?'

'No,' said Daphne, 'but . . .'

'Doesn't matter much. Most of the ones who meet the convoys speak some English. They're naval officers mostly. Dress more or less like ours. Blue uniform, peaked caps. Just walk up to the nearest one and say that Frank sent you.'

She was bubbling with excitement, thanksgiving, pride, political fervour. She looked hard at him and said, 'I don't know how to thank you, Frank.'

'Yes, you do,' said Frank.

This time she opened her eyes occasionally, and didn't think of the Comintern.

On the following day Frank unlocked the door, pecked her on the cheek and said goodbye. She waited impatiently until the estimated half hour was up, opened the door and peered out. there was no one in sight. She went along a corridor, found a ladder and climbed it. Two more corridors, two more ladders, brought her to a stretch of deck with a railing to one side. She followed the railing. there was the gangway. An indifferent looking seaman stood at the top of it. He ignored her. She ignored him. She walked down, stepped on to a worn, concrete surface, and, in a brief moment of exaltation, knelt down to kiss it. Then she rose to her feet, glanced about her, and saw two blue-uniformed figures standing at a trestle table. She made her way to them. She looked joyfully at the elder, obviously more senior one, and said simply, 'Frank sent me.'

'Did he then?' said the younger man, irritably.

Things seemed to be going slightly awry. Perhaps their English wasn't as good as Frank had suggested that it was.

'Frank,' she said, mouthing the words slowly. 'He sent me. From the Party. to Russia.'

The two officers exchanged glances. The elder one spoke.

'I don't know anything about Frank, whoever he is,' he said. 'And I don't know anything about a party. And thank Christ I've never been to Russia. What I *do* know is that you've held up us two customs officers from going home to our breakfasts in Birkenhead, and that you're the last passenger off the Dublin ferry.'

A KISS IS STILL A KISS

SERGEANT Ron Baker had never given much thought to Americans. To his mind they were what you saw at the cinema. Deanna Durbin, Mickey Rooney, James Cagney and the rest, behaving entertainingly and living rather opulently in a country that he didn't want to go to and which was in any case out of his reach.

'Yes, you can tell them back in Oregon that you're staying at a typical English country seat.'

He became more interested in them, obsessed with them, in early 1944, when after two and a half years with the 8th Army in Egypt, Libya, Tunisia and Sicily, he came home to Britain and found one of them in bed with his wife.

Baker became implacable. He started a one-man feud against every American in sight. There were plenty of Americans in sight. Baker's supply of targets seemed to be inexhaustible. Hundreds of thousands of uniformed Americans were in the United Kingdom at the time, waiting, as Baker's division was also waiting, for the invasion of continental Europe.

Baker set himself the aim of hitting them, one by one, usually in pubs. He accepted realistically that he couldn't hit *every* soldier in General Eisenhower's armies, but he drew satisfaction from hitting as many as he could. He was good at it. He had once been the welterweight champion of the Aldershot Command.

His company commander and his colonel were less cheered than was Baker by this vendetta. They found it distressing to have one of their best senior NCOs returned to them repeatedly in the custody of the military or civil police, charged with assault, at a time, prior to the Normandy landings, when good sergeants were at a premium. They reproached him, argued with him, reasoned with him and, inevitably, were forced to discipline him. Within a few short weeks Sergeant Baker regressed to Corporal Baker, to Lance Corporal Baker, to Rifleman Baker. He was confined almost permanently to barracks.

His decline in status was a sad waste of military talent. His company commander, backed by the padre, made a last attempt to persuade Baker that he had hit enough Americans, that he should transfer his bellicose energies back to where they would be more socially productive, to preparing to fight Germans. If Baker would give his personal word not to hit another GI, he was told, his confinement would be lifted, his stripes restored, and he would be put back to doing the job of platoon sergeant that he did so well.

Baker considered it and finally agreed. He was swayed

largely by the arguments of the padre. The padre, in a man-to-man fashion, said that he had no inside information on the matter, but it wouldn't surprise him to hear that Baker's record of marital fidelity in North Africa and Sicily had not been without its blemishes. Human frailty was not a monopoly of lonely United States soldiers away from home and of British wives who had not seen their husbands for years on end. Et cetera. Baker said OK.

Baker held to his pledge, generally speaking, although there was ambiguity about what happened on a railway journey.

There were four characters in the piece: Baker; a healthy-looking GI; a dark-haired killick in the Women's Royal Naval Service and an attractive, fair corporal in the Auxiliary Territorial Service. The compartment of their carriage was on a slow train from Paddington to Plymouth. In the manner of wartime trains it was cold, uncomfortable, far from clean, and with defective lighting.

Things, in the Baker analysis, got off to a bad start when the GI began chatting up the two girls. The GI was harmless enough, but he was persistent, and his persistence led Baker to sullen imaginings about the preliminaries to the seduction of his wife. Baker brooded. He regretted his promise to his company commander. He would probably have broken it on the spot but for the cold reaction of the Wren and of the ATS girl to the GI. They were distantly polite, but so far as was possible ignored him.

The GI was undeterred by this feminine incivility. He continued a heavily humorous commentary upon English weather, food and public transport. He sang snatches of romantic song as made popular by Glenn Miller. He pressed cigarettes and candy on the girls. They declined both, but Baker became angrier by the minute. He had noted the hesitancy of the ATS girl about the cigarette, the Wren's longing look at the candy. Surrender, at least to some degree, seemed to Baker to be only a matter of time.

The GI was crooning a song called 'Stolen Kisses', in what he presumably thought of as a seductive tenor, when the train entered a long tunnel. The compartment's lights were inoperative. There was complete darkness. The GI stopped singing. Other noises developed: a rustle, the sounds of a scuffling movement, the sound of a smacking kiss, the further sound of someone getting a fierce backhander across the chops, a grunt.

When the train came out of the tunnel and into the light again the two girls were sitting decorously in their places. Baker stared out of the window. The GI resentfully mopped blood from a split lip with his handkerchief. For the rest of the journey he neither sang nor spoke. None of the others spoke either. They carried on in silence until they got out of the train at Plymouth.

That evening in the Wrennery the Wren told her friends of an amusing happening in the train on her way down. An amorous GI, taking advantage of a dark spell in a tunnel, had kissed an ATS girl sitting on the other side of the compartment from the Wren. The ATS girl had slapped him resoundingly, to such effect that when light had returned he was seen to be wiping blood from his mouth and to be nursing a lip swollen to the size of a bicycle tyre.

The ATS girl gave *her* friends a similar account, except that in her version there was a transposition among the dramatis personae. She said that it was the Wren who had been unwillingly kissed and who had done the slapping.

The GI, asked by derisive mates to explain the swelling around his mouth, told a fundamentally different story from those of the Wren and of the ATS corporal. He had been minding his own business, he said, sitting in the dark of a tunnel, when some goddam dark horse of a limey sergeant had made a pass at one of two limey service girls travelling in the same compartment. The girl had been stupid enough to assume that it was the GI, not the sergeant, who was getting fresh. She had lashed out defensively, and look what had happened to his goddam lip, not to speak of a tooth that had been loosened. Yes, he had thought of taking on the sergeant, but the guy was a *sergeant*, and a big one at that, and there was no point in risking a stretch in the stockade, particularly since the recent order increasing the penalties for brawling with

Allies had been promulgated.

Sergeant Baker made no mention of the incident to anyone, either that evening or later. In the sergeants' mess he did allow himself some contemplative contentment while he studied the back of his right hand; the hand that he had first kissed noisily in the dark of the compartment and had then used to belt the GI with.

CHANGE AT CREWE

VIRTUE was what Gunner Skinner felt when he showed his leave pass to the military police patrol at Euston station. It was an unusual feeling, exaggerated when he glanced at the station clock and later waved his railway warrant at the not very interested ticket collector at the platform barrier. Skinner, grinning, was on time.

Being on time was something of an achievement. Skinner had been late back to camp, an anti-aircraft battery site near Crewe, for five out of his last six leaves. From one of them he had checked in four days later than he should have checked in. That infringement had cost him his bombardier's stripes. The issue of his leave pass on this occasion had been accompanied by a ferociously expressed warning from his battery sergeant-major. The days of leniency were over. If Skinner were late just one more time, the BSM said, he need expect neither sympathy nor mercy. The battery commander would send him down for twenty-eight days in the glasshouse, no error.

Virtuous Skinner had arrived so early that he found an empty seat in a compartment in a carriage near the engine. He stowed his rifle and his equipment on the luggage rack, unbuttoned the clips at the collar of his battledress blouse, and lit a Woodbine, complacently.

The complacency flourished until the ticket-collector arrived. Wrong train, son, he said. This one went non-stop to Lime Street, Liverpool. It did not stop at Crewe, it had never been intended to stop at Crewe, and if Skinner hadn't been so dozey he would have checked in advance that it didn't stop at Crewe. He would have to come back to Crewe on the seven ten

91

from Lime Street on the following morning. That was all there was to say about it, except that since Skinner's railway warrant was made out for a journey to Crewe and he'd now gone in for a ride to Liverpool, he owed the London, Midland and Scottish Railway for the bit in between. That would be five and fourpence.

Skinner paid up wordlessly. He thought about his immediate future. His leave pass expired at 2359 hours. Given his record, no excuse would be accepted or believed. The glasshouse loomed. He sat in hopeless misery, staring resentfully at the other people in the by now packed compartment, mostly sailors returning to their ships. They were ignorant of, indifferent to, his sorrows. They slumbered with open mouths, one of them snoring irritatingly.

Skinner went forlornly to the corridor. He gazed at the accumulating gloom of a late November afternoon, and reflected bitterly upon his predicament. The ticket collector, passing by on some uncompleted railway profit-making business, stopped to chat. He was more affable than he had been at their previous discussion.

Gunners, eh? he said. He'd been one himself in the last do. So, by coincidence, had been the driver and the guard. They often talked about the old days in France. Bloody awful it had been really, but one thing you couldn't forget was the comradeship. All for one and one for all. That was how it was. Same for Skinner's lot, he supposed.

Skinner said savagely that he supposed it was. It would be no bad thing, he added, if some of the comradely solidarity were to be passed down from generation to generation. He was headed for the glasshouse unless he got back to camp on time. What about some old gunners doing a good turn for a young gunner in trouble and stopping the bloody train at Crewe? What about less sentimental talk and more practical help?

The ticket-collector tut-tutted. He said that that was impossible, and Skinner knew it. You couldn't muck about with trains. He nodded goodbye, and moved on, towards the engine. He came back ten minutes later. Skinner, generating despondency, was still in the corridor.

Don't get too optimistic, the ticket-collector said, but he'd just had a quiet word with the driver. The driver was willing to stretch a point to lend a hand to somebody in the Royal Regiment in difficulties. He couldn't actually *stop* the train at Crewe, but he could slow it and still meet his scheduled arrival time at Lime Street by picking up a bit of speed here and there. It wouldn't be all that slow at Crewe, mind, but if Skinner were prepared to jump and to risk breaking a leg or something, the driver would do his best. OK by Skinner?

Skinner, thinking grimly of that fearsome glasshouse, said that it was OK by him. Just tell him when to get ready.

The getting ready took place two hours later. Skinner by then had had time to think. He didn't much like his thoughts, which resolved themselves into a choice of unpleasant alternatives. Twenty-eight days in the glasshouse or broken bones? Which was worse? The glasshouse, by Skinner's reckoning.

He tried to reassure himself about the jump. He was fit and reasonably athletic, and might even be said to be experienced, to the extent that in his civilian past he had tried to impress girls, and had annoyed tram and bus conductors, by leaping from the platforms of public vehicles well before they reached their authorized stops. He knew the technique. Unless you wanted to fall flat on your face you sprinted from the moment that your feet first hit the ground, and decelerated until your legs were under proper control.

In this particular case, however, there would be complications. From what the ticket-collector had said it was clear that the train would be moving faster than had any vehicle from which Skinner had ever jumped before. He would be unbalanced by the need to wear his pack and webbing equipment. He would have a rifle to carry. There was no point in risking injury to avoid a charge of Absent Without Leave if he had to face another one probably more serious, of losing his kit and his weapon.

The door, heavy and hinged on its forward side, was an impediment that had worried him too, but the ticket-collector had eased his mind on at least that. Skinner's starting point would be the footplate of the driver's cab. The driver would call out his assessment of the best combination of slow speed and availability of platform length to run along. The ticket-collector would act as despatcher.

Skinner went edgily to the cab. It was hot and noisy. Outside, there was little to see in the blackout. The air rushed by, alarmingly fast. Gradually, imperceptibly, the rush diminished. Skinner rechecked his equipment. Everything buckled and buttoned. Rifle carried at its point of balance. He loosened up with a few knees bends.

The train was slowing noticeably. Not noticeably enough for Skinner's peace of mind. Dimmed lights came into view ahead. The driver was shouting something above the racket of the engine. The ticket-collector motioned to Skinner to take his place on the footplate. Skinner moved down gingerly, clasped a stanchion, looked down at the ground whizzing by, looked up again hastily, and thought God, this thing's still doing about thirty miles per hour.

The end of a station platform came in sight, grew rapidly in size. The driver shouted again. The ticket-collector tapped Skinner on the shoulder and snapped, 'Good luck, son. NOW!' Skinner jumped.

His feet met the station platform with a disorganized clatter, wildly out of control. The impetus seemed to be thrusting his trunk forward faster than his legs could catch up with it. He stumbled, worked his legs violently, righted, stumbled again, righted again and ran, rifle held above his head, faster than he had ever run in his life. He flashed past some bedraggled advertisements and a sign saying 'Crewe'. He felt a developing control over his legs, a synchronization of muscle and sinew. A huge sense of delight possessed him. No broken bones. No glasshouse. Must keep running though, slow methodically if he wasn't to fall.

He saw two red-capped military policemen ahead of him. They turned when they heard the quick hammering of his boots on the platform. They looked at him, and looked at the train thundering through the station. It was gathering speed. The military policemen crouched a little as Skinner sprinted towards them. They braced themselves, caught him in full flight and staggered.

They wasted no time. The guard's van of the train, its sliding doors open, came abreast of them two seconds after they had body-checked Skinner. They picked him up as if he were a sack of mail and threw him vigorously into the van.

'Just made it, mate,' he heard one of them bawling as he sped in the direction of Liverpool. 'If it hadn't been for us you'd have overstayed your leave.'

CORRESPONDING WAYS

AMONG European armies, the British is the only one that for over nine hundred years has not had to conduct major operations against a foreign invader on its home territory. There has been some domestic fighting since Hastings in 1066, but aside from a brief and insignificant French incursion to a remote part of Pembrokeshire in Napoleonic times, it has been internecine and dynastic, and a long time ago. Excluding Ireland, 13/16ths* of which ceased to be British in 1921, Zeppelin raids in the First World War, and more dangerous *Luftwaffe* bombing in the Second, the British civilian experience of warfare has been secondhand. The pub bores who once reminisced endlessly about their exciting experiences during the Wars of the Roses, or the battle of Naseby, or the Monmouth Rebellion, or the '45, are long since dead and forgotten.

This immunity from local destruction, a product of life on the right side of a saltwater moat dominated efficiently (usually) by the Royal Navy, gave to British armies down the generations characteristics unique among their contemporaries. For one thing, it was easier for the soldiers, and for those British civilians who took an interest in what they were up to, to take a detached view of the effects of military proceedings when the towns and villages pillaged and wrecked, the crops ruined and the non-combatants accidentally slaughtered or starved to death, belonged to somebody else. For another, the

* Calculated by counties, not by head of population or square mile of land, in case anyone wants to get argumentative.

commanders and the commanded were not performing under the critical scrutiny of an audience of their compatriots.

A consequence of this second consideration was that the home spectators, so to speak, drew their knowledge of the army's progress from reportage, unalloyed by observation. For several centuries the generals held a reporting monopoly. They sent despatches describing their achievements or, when necessary, throwing the blame for their failures on somebody else. When, as frequently happened, the despatches or a version of them fell into the hands of imaginative poets, there was apt to be an element of patriotic distortion. The poets, none of whom had personal experience of anything resembling the events that they were commemorating, put out rousing stuff about such unusual battlefield orders from a general officer as: 'Once more unto the breach, dear friends' (W. Shakespeare), and such unlikely sentiments from troops committed to an ill-organized fiasco as: 'Theirs not to reason why' (A. Tennyson). The less said about the promotion prospects of the subaltern who, finding himself hampered by a dead colonel, a jammed Gatling and a ferocious crowd of the enemy closing upon his position, advised his platoon of Victorian hard cases to 'Play up! play up! and play the game!' (W. Henley) the better. This romanticism much inspired the British public.

Matters began to change in the middle part of the nineteenth century, when the first properly accredited war correspondent, Mr William Russell, was sent by the London *Times* to the Crimean War. Mr Russell took a jaundiced view of a great deal of what he saw, and said so in print to an increasingly literate British newspaper-reading public. He was notably critical of the calamitous inadequacies of the medical and supply arrangements. His accounts stimulated an upheaval that led to the arrival in Scutari of Florence Nightingale who permanently reformed army nursing, some improvement in the forwarding and distribution of clothing suitable to a Russian winter, and extensive unpopularity for Mr Russell among the commanders on the spot and with their superiors at the Horse Guards.

Judged by the standards of his day, Mr Russell's interventions were revolutionary. But he remained to some extent a prisoner of contemporary conventions. He looked upon patently bad practices as fair targets for his attacks. He was more restrained about patently incompetent people. To a later generation of his readers this seems a pity. He had some rich material at his disposal.

Any modern war correspondent would have had a high old time, for example, with the command structure of the army as then constituted. At home the commander-in-chief shared the attitudes of his successor, the Duke of Cambridge, who summarized his organizational doctrine as: 'The right time to make a change is when you cannot help it.' One of the changes that he had been able to help not making was the introduction of a retiring age for senior officers. When the Crimean War began, the active list included thirteen generals with more than seventy years' service, thirty-seven with between sixty and seventy years and one hundred and sixty-three with between fifty and sixty years. Lord Raglan, who commanded in the field, had last been in action at Waterloo nearly forty years previously and habitually referred to the enemy as 'the French', an idiosyncrasy that upset General Canrobert, Raglan's French ally, who thought that he had come to collaborate with Raglan against the Russians.

At Inkerman, a battle won entirely because of the quality of the junior officers and the soldiers, one general brought up his division to support another beset by Russians. The disposition of the reinforcements was settled with a courteous simplicity that cut staffwork to a minimum.

'Where do you want me to place my division?' asked the first.

'Anywhere you like, my dear sir,' said the second.

Russell left a veil discreetly over this sort of thing, as he did over the cause of the Light Cavalry Brigade being put into a suicidally gallant attack against the wrong objective. His successors in later Victorian wars became slowly, tentatively, more outspoken. It was a long time before a healthy cooperation with the press became regarded as a necessary component of generalship.

By the time of the South African war at the turn of the century, the generals by and large accepted the presence of correspondents upon their battlefields with a suspicious wariness that occasionally reached a peak of begrudging tolerance. Rudyard Kipling and Conan Doyle got some help because they were eminent as writers and powerful enough to raise merry hell if they were treated with too little consideration. Winston Churchill, abominated as a pushing young know-all who alternated between holding a commission in the 4th Hussars and taking leave to write tendentious and self-glorifying commentaries on campaigns conducted by his professional seniors, was tolerated because he was the son of a Duke and nobody could do much about that.

The old spirit lingered on, however, particularly in the breast of Lord Kitchener, who commanded the army during the last phase, prolonged, of the war. His way with press conferences was a model that must excite envy among many a modern VIP accosted at airports by television interviewers and required by custom to give the nation an account of his recent activities.

The correspondents who assembled at Southampton for a statement by the victor were dispersed by a roar of 'Get out of my way, you drunken swabs,' followed by the silent departure of the hero to his train.

PRESS ON THROUGH THE SMOKE

THERE was a massive change in British social attitudes between 1918 and 1939. Disillusionment and cynicism with national leaders, political and military, had flowed from a counting of the appalling 1914-18 casualty totals, mass unemployment, an international economic slump and the government's inability to contain resurgent German aggression. The Labour Party had displaced the Liberals as the alternative to the Conservatives, had briefly been in power, and less briefly had shared power in a coalition administration. The press reflected, and to some degree directed, popular unwillingness to accept for much longer traditional rigidities of class and rank that had prevailed for centuries.

When the Second World War began the citizen soldiers who expanded around the nucleus of the small interwar regular army were better educated, more sceptical and less inclined to respond unquestioningly to orders for no other reason than that they were orders. Commanders who wanted the best from them soon found that the way to get it was to treat the troops as intelligent collaborators, not as mindless yes-men. It was far from a new philosophy. Many of the up-and-coming younger officers had been preaching it and practising it for some years.

Its prime, and ultimately most influential exemplar, started the war as a major general commanding the 2nd Division and ended it as Field Marshal the Viscount Montgomery of Alamein. His detractors, particularly those among the many senior officers whom he sacked, assiduously put it about that he was an egotistical, self-advertising little upstart. This was almost entirely true, but he was also a deep-thinking, highly professionally educated military technician who, with the one aberration of Arnhem, never lost a battle. He came to the Western Desert at a time when British winners were thin on the ground. A conversation overheard soon after his arrival was:

'What's the new man like?'

'He's an efficient shit.'

'Thank Christ for that.'

To technical virtuosity and a cavalier ruthlessness in discarding subordinate commanders who came under his portmanteau heading of 'useless', Montgomery added a policy, practised by others elsewhere but not previously with the elaboration put into it by him, of making himself personally known to as many as possible of the soldiers he led.

Because he had studied and thought about it, he had a deep awareness of the value of publicity to the morale of a mid-twentieth-century army manned almost entirely by transmogrified civilians from an advanced industrial society. Whenever it was practicable Montgomery, on his excursions to chat up the soldiery, was accompanied by press correspondents, newsreel cameramen and BBC wireless commentators. He, and the 8th Army, accordingly became known by appearance as well as by achievement to the home public with an intimacy never before approached by an army or commander in British history. The personal side of all this advertising caused much deep breathing in traditionalist circles, and no distress whatsoever to Montgomery himself.

The technique used by him in these forays to the troops had to be adapted to circumstances, but was basically consistent. Units paraded formally for his inspection were invited to break ranks, gather round and listen to him. From the front of a jeep, or from some similar improvised rostrum, he would tell them in simple terms, heavily larded with sporting metaphors, about what he intended to do to the enemy and about what he expected from his audience. Bodies of other troops, not paraded but going up the line, training or working on blown bridges or mined tracks anywhere from Egypt to Italy, were apt to find themselves being given crisp words of encouragement from an athletic little man wearing two cap badges and a comfortably unmilitary outfit of a rollneck sweater, slacks and, in season, a sheepskin jacket.

Informality of dress was part of the mystique. Montgomery was impatiently dismissive of the conventions of soldierly turnout, although he once in Sicily took exception to a Canadian bulldozer driver dressed in a looted top hat and nothing else. (The bulldozer driver didn't improve things by raising the hat, bowing, and addressing the Army Commander as 'Boss'.)

Another component of the procedure was the distribution of cigarettes. The general was a man of austere personal habits, and among the several things that he didn't do was smoke. He did not let private disinclination interfere with public relations. Since most of his soldiers seemed to like smoking, and since Montgomery had access to unlimited supplies of free issue cigarettes, army morale and the Montgomery reputation benefited mutually from an order to the ADC to keep his general's vehicle well stocked with smokes.

A wayside off-the-cuff oration, followed by the handing over in person of successive tins of fifty, went down well and was often suitably recorded on camera and described in print and on the air. For at least one 8th Army soldier this form of largesse caused a misunderstanding about what generals were for. It also demonstrated that public relations campaigns, like all campaigns, have their limitations, however expertly the research has been carried out.

In early 1944 General Montgomery returned from Italy to Britain to take up his new job as ground commander of the British, American and Canadian armies preparing for the landings in Northwest Europe. He departed in a widespread limelight of publicity, and his new appointment was headline news throughout the English-speaking world. His successor in Italy was General Sir Oliver Leese.

General Leese was a large, tidy officer from the Brigade of Guards who operated effectively, dressed conventionally and was not much given to gimmicks. He had so far got along very well without them. It was suggested to him by his staff that now that he had inherited the Montgomery mantle, a few extrovert gestures as made by his predecessor might help to perpetuate the formidably successful spirit and legend of the 8th Army. A programme of this sort did not come naturally to General Leese, but he agreed to give it a try. The press and the BBC were briefed appropriately.

The general intended to start in a small way with a round trip by jeep embracing a series of extempore chats with groups of troops met on the way, each chat to be complemented by an issue of cigarettes. The general's little convoy set out. The correspondents followed. They kept clear of the talking. Their idea was to put some questions to those who had been addressed after the general had moved on, with a view to finding out how well the venture had gone down.

The first man they spoke to was a grizzled sapper, one of a party who had been at work on road maintenance. He was lighting up appreciatively when the press group reached him. Asked for his impressions of the new management he drew reflectively on his cigarette and gave them.

'There was another bloke used to come round handing out fags,' he said, 'but he must have moved on somewhere else.'

THE REHABILITATION OF
PRIVATE McCLUNG

NEITHER the first nor the last British commander to undergo the experience, Lieutenant General Neil Ritchie suffered defeat in the Western Desert at the hands of General Erwin Rommel of the Afrika Korps. General Ritchie, a striking looking general, was the youngest commander that 8th Army had ever had. At the time of his first appointment the press had imaginatively, and embarrassingly, endowed him in print with gifts that he did not possess and did not claim to possess.

When he was relieved of his command in 1941 there was thus even more public interest in what had gone wrong than would normally have been the case. He continued to be one of the small handful of British generals who, in the pre-Montgomery-public-relations-machine era, was recognizable by appearance, or known by reputation, to everyone in the United Kingdom who read a newspaper.

At the same time as General Ritchie was in the process of transfer to a less demanding job in Scottish Command, another military transaction was concluded between two establishments several miles distant from one another on the outskirts of Glasgow. Private McClung, looking uncharacteristically smart, fit, burnished and blancoed, and also looking characteristically resentful, was on his way back to his recruit depot after completing a sentence of twenty-eight days' detention in a military prison. It had been his third stretch. Despite its rigours, McClung could still be said to be ahead on points.

What Rommel had been to Ritchie so, on a less elevated stratum, was McClung to every one of those superiors appointed by the army to oversee him.

At the time there were, by the nature of things, a great many reluctant soldiers in a huge, conscripted wartime army. Almost all of these adapted to the inevitable with varying degrees of resignation. McClung wasn't interested in adaptability, and he was unfamiliar with resignation. He simply objected strongly to the whole thing. He was uninhibited, fearless, impetuous, single-minded and physically strong. He was early labelled a disruptive influence. He rapidly moved up the classifications until he became a registered bloody nuisance.

Regular NCOs who thought that they knew a thing or two about how to deal with the likes of McClung soon acknowledged that they were on to something new. McClung argued angrily, countered reproof with insult, disputed most orders, refused to obey others and when he ran out of his limited supply of words with which to express his interminable objections to military life, clouted his opponents regardless of occasion or rank. It was as the consequence of three of these resorts to grievous bodily harm, one a spectacular technical knock-out of a corporal during the adjutant's parade, that McClung had put in his three stretches, total eighty-four days, in the glasshouse. On the day of his completion of the last one his overall time in the King's uniform, glasshouse interludes included, was four months.

Had he been in, say, the German, Russian or Japanese armies he would have been dealt with in a manner that his present superiors regretted wistfully was not open to them. Instead, what was known unofficially as the McClung committee was set up to investigate all aspects of the McClung problem, and to make recommendations for its solution. The committee's chairman was the adjutant. Its members were McClung's company commander, his company sergeant-major, the padre and a psychiatrist, a temporary employee of the Royal Army Medical Corps.

Before it got down to work it was made clear to the

committee that the simple option of discharging McClung from the army as unemployable was out. If McClung got away with it, others would try. The whole structure of compulsory national service would be at risk. Conversely, it was accepted that the current repetitive sequence of confrontation, violence, arrest and detention, could not be allowed to continue. It was too wasteful of time, manpower and money, and was damaging to the morale of the other recruits. Within these defined boundaries the committee would have to think of something, fast.

After long consideration of a spread of not very helpful suggestions – try to transfer McClung to the navy, send him down the mines, accidentally shoot the bugger (the CSM's offering), parachute him into Germany, persuade the medical officer to keep him under permanent sedation – the buck was passed to the psychiatrist and the padre. McClung, it was agreed without much hope, needed psychotherapeutic and spiritual help.

Following extensive interviews with McClung, individually and jointly conducted, the psychiatrist and the padre made their recommendation. It was founded upon the premise that since McClung was untrainable as an infantry soldier, and since for reasons of higher policy it had been laid down that he must be retained on the strength and in uniform, an identifiably worthwhile job must be found for him that would give him a sense of pride and fulfilment and at the same time subject him to the least possible exposure to the more niggling exigencies of formal military discipline. In short, it was advisable to make him feel *wanted*.

These findings were met with some cynicism, particularly from the company sergeant-major. It was decided to try to implement them as the least hopeless of a set of hopeless horrible options. By good chance a possible niche for McClung in his new experimental role was found to be immediately available.

A row of six detached brick barrackrooms, built by a contractor to replace six dilapidated Nissen huts dating from the First World War, had recently been completed. Five of the

, six were in occupation, their internal furnishings and external surrounds kept to a high state of cleanliness by their recruit occupants, supervised by the trained soldiers who were responsible for each hut. The sixth was, for the moment, uninhabitable. The contractor had botched his job. There were leaks in the roof. The drainage from around the other five huts was so defective that in wet weather the sixth was partially flooded. Its woodwork had been left unpainted. Jumbled heaps of builders' rubble and miscellaneous junk littered the ground outside.

McClung was put in sole charge of tidying up this malfunctioning eyesore. How he did it, he was told, was up to him. All that was required was that it should be done. A wheelbarrow and tools were put at his disposal. He could indent for any necessary additional stores through the company quartermaster sergeant. There was brief doubt about whether McClung might refuse to have anything to do with it, but he allayed it dourly. He'd do it, he said. Further doubts, about how effectively he would do it, and for how long, stayed active. Only the padre showed qualified optimism.

There was surprise and pleasure when it was seen how McClung got down to work. He started with the rubble. Within two days he had cleared it, and stacked it in two neat piles at the back of the hut. He moved next to the drainage. He did some brief surveying, dug a sloped trench across the space that lay between his hut and the next one, lined the trench with rubble from one of his piles, and pointed the outlet towards waste ground. It rained hard two days after he had finished this. No floodwater affected McClung's hut. Some rain came through the holes in the roof, but he clambered about and fixed them too.

He next turned his attentions to painting. The CQMS gave him brushes and tins of paint. McClung worked stolidly for ten days. The woodwork, inside and out, shone glossily with a white finish.

The company commander was delighted with the exertions of this new McClung, but became worried at the speed with which he was dealing with everything, and the competence with which he did it. There would soon be nothing left for him to do. What would happen then?

McClung, his teeth well into his task, was by no means finished with it. From his second stack of rubble he built a fancily laid bricked path, that joined the barrack hut doorway to the adjacent metalled road. This done, he moved on to gardening. He cleared, dug over, weeded and raked to a fine tilth the soil in front of, to both sides and behind the hut. There was a potentially ugly moment when the CQMS, momentarily forgetful of the purpose of the enterprise, said curtly that he ran a quartermaster's store, not a bloody nursery garden, and bloody grass seed was not on his inventory, but fortunately the company commander overheard the argument. He placated McClung and bought grass seed privately. McClung sowed his lawns, protected the seeds against birds by criss-crossing the earth with a network of string fastened to low sticks, and indented for further seeds of different types.

The CQMS, abashed by his previous indiscretion, at once referred McClung to the company commander, who saw a fine opportunity to keep the whole thing going. He invested extravagantly in a comprehensive selection of seeds, bulbs, seedlings, shoots and gardening implements. That lot, he calculated, should keep McClung occupied for months to come.

It did, aided by a happy chance. There was more accommodation in the depot than was needed by the recruit intakes who reported in at intervals. McClung's hut did not have to be put to its proper use. It became undisputed McClung territory. He brushed and dusted the inside, and polished the windows. Outside he cut his grass, and tended his geraniums, petunias, phlox, gladioli and the rest. It was not the sort of employment that would have commended itself to military manpower planners, but it kept McClung out of trouble, kept a great many other people from having to deal with the outcome of the trouble and solved an unusual problem unconventionally. Also, the end-product looked good.

The end-product looked so good that the company commander decided to show it off at a forthcoming general's inspection. He also, primed by the padre who had kept a kindly pastoral eye on the experiment and who was in periodic consultation with the psychiatrist about it, had a long private talk with McClung. He hoped, said the company commander, that experience had demonstrated to McClung that the army was a flexible organization, scrupulous in the search for square holes into which square pegs, previously inserted into round ones, could be resited. The army was always anxious to develop latent talent, self-expression, and the promotion of socially useful projects, however unorthodox. There was a lot more of this sort of stuff, followed by the punchline. If McClung would guarantee to restore his standard of personal turnout which, frankly, had deteriorated recently doubtless because of the nature of his – er – duties, to the peak that it had achieved on the day when he had been sprung from the military prison, the company commander would have him paraded outside his exemplary barrack hut and attractive attached garden for commendation to, and doubtless congratulation by General Ritchie. General Ritchie would be inspecting the depot on the following Tuesday.

The benefit that McClung had drawn from the understanding consideration with which he had been treated was now displayed movingly. He said quietly and humbly that he was grateful for all that had been done for him. He much appreciated the suggestion that he should meet General Ritchie. It would be an honour. As for his personal turn-out, there need be no worry. He would be as spick and span as a guardsman at the Trooping of the Colour.

On the Tuesday morning McClung, a model of soldierly sartorial perfection, Glengarry brushed and at the correct angle, brasses glittering, boots gleaming, knife-edged creases in his battledress trousers, stood smartly at ease in front of his trimmed lawn. He was surrounded by riotously colourful banks of flowers in weeded beds, and backed by the flawless paintwork on the window fixtures of his scrubbed and dusted barrackroom.

From the corner of his eye he saw the inspection party approaching, General Ritchie in front wearing a red-banded cap and red tabs at his collar. McClung recognized him at once, from old newsreels and newspaper photographs. The general kept pointing with his swagger stick and being shown things, and asking questions and getting answers.

McClung was glad to note that the general was thorough. He went into each of the other five barrackrooms in turn, followed by the entourage. From the time he spent in each it was evident that few details were left unlooked into. Well, however good the others were, and McClung conceded to himself that some of them weren't bad, they weren't in the same class as his was. He saw General Ritchie come out of the next-door one. McClung crashed to attention and stared straight ahead.

He heard the general's voice clearly. 'I think that that's enough barrackrooms,' General Ritchie said, 'they're all in top-class condition. I've no doubt the rest are too. Let's take a look at your cookhouse.'

McClung, still rigidly at attention, moved his eyes. The party was walking *away* from him.

They soon all turned round though. McClung had a carrying voice, especially when he was set on making it carry. He helped it by cupping his hands to his mouth.

'Send for fucking Rommel,' roared McClung, in a combination of rage, disappointment and disillusionment.

'And where are your buckets of sand for incendiaries?'

REVERSE CHARGE

THE pre-1914 Imperial German Staff, who were famously both systematic and analytical, produced among much else of military interest some crisp guidance upon how the performance and potential of officers should be assessed.

Four basic qualities were subdivided into two sets of antitheses: intelligence and stupidity, energy and idleness. Experience, suggested the staff study, demonstrated that various combinations from each of these sets produced consistent patterns from which conclusions could be drawn.

A stupid and energetic officer was an appalling nuisance who should be got rid of as soon as possible.

A stupid and idle officer did little harm, and so long as his senior NCOs were up to their jobs could safely be promoted eventually to the command of a company. But no further.

An intelligent and energetic officer should be encouraged in every way, and should be marked for early advancement. Ultimately he would make an excellent chief of staff.

An intelligent and idle officer was destined for the very top, an army commander at the least. He would not be bogged down in necessary but mind-clouding detail, which he would idly and intelligently delegate to the reliable hands of his chief of staff.

Chetwynd's colonel, when contemplating Chetwynd in the light of this German analysis, reflected gloomily that the accuracy of its thinking was flawed by the confident extravagance of that one of its recommendations relevant to Chetwynd. Chetwynd was stupid and energetic, and was an appalling nuisance, but it was impossible in the late spring of 1944 to get rid of him. The colonel had tried, repeatedly. He had been rebuffed, repeatedly. With the largest amphibious operation in history, the Normandy landings, in the final phase of preparation the resources of British manpower were stretched to their elastic limits. Chetwynd was irreplaceable because here were no trained available replacements for a subaltern in an Armoured Car Regiment. A reinforcement pool of young officers existed, but its role was to provide substitutes for future casualties, not for presently active commissioned halfwits.

The colonel wondered from time to time about the Germanic prototypes who had inspired the author of the study. Simply by relating them in his mind to Chetwynd he could develop a clear picture of what they looked like, how they spoke, how they behaved. They doubtless had bullet heads, thick necks, straight backs, gingery moustaches and a habit of hurrying officiously wherever they went with grim, soldierly expressions on their witless faces, issuing curt reproaches, interfering in matters that had nothing to do with them, enforcing, as they saw it, discipline.

He supposed that they, too, had been self-taught specialists in whatever the German equivalent was of the *Manual of Military Law*. Chetwynd was certainly one in the British version, a heavy, red-bound volume that he was believed to read in bed. It was an obsession that had led to a great deal of trouble for a great many people. The colonel counted himself among the victims. It made him feel impotent and bitter.

Most of the difficulties with Chetwynd derived from this book. He was a persistent putter of soldiers on charges. Many were for familiar, recognizable illegalities. Others, the trickier ones, were concerned with authentic but esoteric offences that neither Chetwynd's squadron commander nor the colonel had ever heard of. Queried about these whilst giving evidence, Chetwynd would demoralize his seniors by quoting the precise subparagraph that defined them, adding a respectfully partronizing commentary for the laity, and offering helpful advice on related aspects of military jurisprudence that they might profitably look up. He compounded his unpopularity by always being right.

On several occasions his squadron commander, and on two occasions the colonel, had urged Chetwynd to moderation in his pursuit of transgressors. Soldiers who should have been concentrating upon last-minute details of their preparations for the onslaught on continental Europe were wasting their time, the time of NCOs who had to give evidence, and the time of officers who had to hear the cases, in arguing the toss about whether While On Active Service their berets had been adjusted to an incorrect angle, or the truth of the accusation that they had failed to salute an American second-lieutenant who was passing by in a jeep.

No one was suggesting, it was put to Chetwynd, that the whole, traditional apparatus of military law should be dismantled and put into suspension. What was being suggested, and suggested pretty forcefully, was that the application of a little less nit-picking zeal, and of a little more applied commonsense, would contribute constructively to the successful completion of the task to which the Regiment was committed across the English Channel.

Chetwynd was unpersuaded. He didn't see it like that at all, he said. He would of course continue to obey without question all lawful orders given to him by his superior officers but he had no latitude in his interpretation of the measures necessary to preserve discipline. Selectivity was a non-starter. The functions that he discharged were entrusted to him as mandatory duties enshrined in the Army Act. He was reluctant to exercise his right, spelled out explicitly in paragraph something that neither the colonel nor the squadron commander subsequently bothered to check, to appeal to higher authority about what, with renewed respect, seemed to be a proposal that he should conspire to break the law by calculated omissions to preserve it, but if . . . All right, they said wearily.

The straw that broke the colonel's back was to do with tyres. At that time normally honest men, some of senior rank, connived at or instigated a specialized form of theft. Motor

113

tyres were in limited supply. A unit's success in the coming fighting, and the personal survival of some of its members, might depend upon the durability of the tyres of its wheeled vehicles. Armoured cars, scout cars, three-tonners, fifteen-hundredweights, jeeps that had been put to long mileages in repeated exercises and bore tyres approaching baldness were a threat to both success and survival.

What started as a few opportunist switchings of wheels with those of vehicles belonging to somebody else and left temporarily unattended, soon swelled into planned raids on vehicle parks. Outright larceny was regarded as anti-social. A straight swap of indifferent for good was acceptable.

A corollary of unauthorized acquisition was the safeguarding of the acquired. Commanding officers ordered that no vehicle, anywhere, in any circumstances, should ever be left untended. Vehicle park sentries were double and treble-banked. Some COs, including Chetwynd's, took out further insurance. They ordained that all tyres should have painted on them the numbers of the vehicles that they belonged to.

In less exacting times the order would simply have been transmitted through the adjutant in Daily Orders, passed down through squadron commanders to troop commanders, and implemented by drivers under the supervision of NCOs. On this occasion all the officers were committed to more pressing matters. The colonel and his second-in-command had been bidden to a non-smoking, coughing-prohibited exposition by General Montgomery about his immediate plans, an event at which the colonel carefully counted the number of references to God and cricket. The more of these there were, the colonel had deduced from experience in the Western Desert and in Italy, the more hairy was the forthcoming operation likely to be. The other officers went to a demonstration staged by the RAF of the tank-busting proper-ties of rocket-firing Typhoons. Chetwynd, alone, was left to mind the shop.

He was handed a copy of Daily Orders, and told to oversee the tyre painting.

When the colonel, still preoccupied with God and cricket,

returned he found that seventeen drivers were on charges of disobeying a direct order. The order, a quotation from Daily Orders read by Chetwynd to a parade that he had summoned was: 'All tyres will forthwith be painted on top of their sidewalls with the number of the vehicle to which they belong.' Chetwynd explained that he had added an oral supplement. Once NCOs were satisfied that the work had been properly done, the vechicles were to be driven to the front of the Orderly Room where Chetwynd would inspect them. It was during these inspections that he had identified the offences.

The seventeen delinquents had erred on two counts. Not only had the numbers on their tyres been painted at the bottom, instead of at the top, as ordered. They had been painted upside down.

It had at once become evident to Chetwynd that this was an act of collective defiance, amounting to mutiny. But, he said, looking as if he expected to be congratulated, he had borne in mind recent suggestions made by the colonel about leniency and had preferred only the lesser charges of individual disobedience.

The colonel walked wordlessly away.

The colonel passed a disturbed night, dreaming fitfully of the practicalities and possible consequences of murdering Chetwynd by a variety of means.

On the following morning the quartermaster requested a formal interview with his commanding officer. When the quartermaster was formal he was very formal. The colonel had known him since his enlistment as a trooper in 1928. He saluted whippily, and with a grave expression on his face said that he had put Chetwynd under close arrest on a charge of sexual perversion, i.e. indecent exposure.

The colonel looked at him in deadpan silence.

The offence contravened Section whatever it was of the Army Act, went on the quartermaster, glibly. The indecency had been committed outside the officers' mess on the previous evening. The quartermaster had caught him at it red-handed, if that was the right expression. It was the quartermaster's personal opinion that Chetwynd was in need of psychiatric attention rather than punishment. The quartermaster understood that psychiatric examination was a long process. A very long process.

The colonel agreed that it was, he had always heard, a long process. He took immediate steps to ensure that Chetwynd would undergo it.

Five weeks later, on an evening when regimental headquarters was established in a damaged Norman farmhouse outside Bayeux, and after the quartermaster had brought up and distributed several jeeploads of replenishment ammunition and rations, the colonel sociably broke out his whisky. He poured a large tot for the quartermaster, and another for himself, and the two of them became relaxed and confidential. Talk turned to the pre-landing past. which in view of recent happenings seemed a very long time ago.

'Did you make that up about Chetwynd?' said the colonel suddenly, abruptly.

'No. It was true, He *did* expose himself.'

'Just like that?'

'Well, not quite just like that. It cost me six pints in the mess. Three for him and three for me. I'd told the mess sergeant to lock the loo door and put an out-of-order notice on it. When Chetwynd went outside I followed and . . .'

'I see,' said the colonel.

Later he said, 'Thanks, Bill.'

I DON'T LIKE YOUR MANNA

THE relationship between a Balkan guerrilla leader and the British liaison officer parachuted in to support him was not infrequently beset by complexities over which the liaison officer had no control. Their resolution required a delicacy of touch.

The delicacy of Colonel S. W. Bailey's touch kept getting jerked out of true by somebody on his own side, working a long way away. This person was responsible for the selection and packing of the contents of stores canisters, flown by RAF aircraft from North Africa and dropped over Yugoslavia to chosen reception areas delineated by signal fires laid out in an agreed pattern and tended by Chetniks.

The distribution of these stores gave Bailey his strongest bargaining counter. They were influential currency in his otherwise not very satisfactory attempts to persuade General Draža Mihajlović, the Chetnik commander, to modify his policies.

The prime difficulty about these negotiations was an incompatibility of interests between what Bailey was instructed to urge Mihajlović to do, and what Mihajlović conceived it as his duty to do.

Bailey's brief was to induce Mihajlović to use his Chetniks to fight more Germans than they so far had done, and to devote less of their energies and ammunition to trying to shoot their fellow countrymen, Tito's Communist-led Partisans, who were fighting Germans much more seriously than the Chetniks were. If the Chetniks and Partisans could be argued into burying their differences and into operating jointly

*'H.Q., Sir? Round the corner and the second building on
the right; you can't mistake it, it's camouflaged.'*

against the Germans, consequent German entanglements
would diminish the size of Axis reinforcements available to
counter planned Anglo–American ventures in Italy, thus
benefiting the overall Allied cause.

Mihajlović saw the prospects differently. He was a Serbian
monarchist, a regular officer with constitutional and personal
responsibilities towards the young King Peter. The weight of
these responsibilities had been added to by Mihajlović's
appointment by the Royal Yugoslav government in exile as

118

Minister for War. As he viewed it, his proper role was not to take premature action against the Germans. There would be too little gain at too much cost. The right course was to husband his resources, organize a large guerrilla force, and to put it to really active use only in conjunction with a major Allied landing on the Adriatic coast.

In the meanwhile Mihajlović considered that there was a pressing domestic problem to be solved. The greatest existing threat to the restoration of the monarchical *status quo ante bellum* was posed by the Communists. Mihajlović was determined to destroy the Partisans before they became too powerful to deal with.

It was a matter of no surprise to Bailey that his discussions with Mihajlović were conducted in no such simple a manner as the tabling of a mutually agreed agenda, the detailed consideration of points of difference and an orderly progression from one item to the next. Bailey had known the Balkans for a long time. Before the war he had for some years worked at the Trepčka mines in Serbia. He was a fluent speaker of Serbo-Croat. He expected strong elements of evasiveness, ambivalence, delay, sensitivity, intrigue and misleading assurance.

He wasn't too put out when General Mihajlović refused to speak to him for days on end, and he accepted with a wry stoicism the Mihajlović system for demonstrating the current Bailey status on the Chetnik popularity graph. When Bailey was in favour, almost invariably after a successful supply drop, he was invited by the general to ride with him at the head of the column. When there had been an unsuccessful drop, or when there was a long interval between drops, Bailey was relegated to the rear among the cooks, baggage and camp followers.

His first intimation that a slap-happy eccentricity had crept into the loading manifests came in response to a request by him for negotiable tender suitable for the payment of Bosnian peasants in exchange for food, shelter, pack-animals and assorted goods and services. Bailey's conviction was that a scrupulous attention to payments would provide evidence of honesty and goodwill, and would inspire local confidence in the probity of the British Mission.

What he was sent to meet this requirement was a consignment of thirteen million Italian East African lire, each note superimposed with the word 'Ethiopia'. There was an accompanying instruction about Bailey's financial obligations. He was told to make a personal physical count of this treasure. His totals were to be cross-checked by his second in command, and he was to signal a certificate of safe delivery and acceptance.

Bailey sensibly ignored both the notes and his auditing duties, but he was soon faced with a fresh problem posed by the arrival from the skies on to a snow-bound Bosnian massif in the depths of winter of heavy stocks of tropical snakebite serum.

These in turn were followed by five hundred left-footed boots, a damaging blow to Bailey's prestige at Chetnik headquarters, which began to look worse when an even larger collection of boots, this time in pairs, turned out all to be size 6. Bailey saved something from the wreckage by claiming ingeniously that this second lot of boots was not, as had originally been thought, intended for some of the largest men with some of the largest feet in Europe, but was indicative of British concern, even at the height of a war, for the plight of the young. He distributed them to children, and won much affection and gratitude as a sort of early precursor of an Oxfam disaster relief administrator.

One promising and potentially valuable load went wrong because, although it was carefully and correctly packed, the phantom sender forgot to signal in advance either what was on the way or how it was marked. Two canisters landed midway between two Chetnik bands whose leaders regarded one another with deep dislike. In one canister were grenades. In the other were their detonator and fuse sets, wrapped about with shock resistant material and kept separate from the grenades during the drop in case after they hit the ground they all went off in one big bang.

A dangerous looking argument between the two leaders in

contention for this prize seemed to be approaching the stage when blood would be spilled, when a compromise was agreed upon. Each band took one canister. This piece of *détente* left the first band with a large quantity of grenades that wouldn't work without detonators, and the other with a similar number of detonators that were worthless because there was nothing to put them into.

And so it went on. In the long run, aside from the effect upon Bailey's internal adrenalin production and distribution, it didn't matter very much. British support was withdrawn from the Chetniks and transferred to the immeasurably more militarily productive Partisans. Bailey's Mission, and its subordinate sub-Missions, was pulled out. Mihajlović, an honourable man who had backed the wrong horse, was captured and shot by the victorious Partisans shortly after the end of the war.

Bailey never identified the capricious consigner who turned most of his airdrops into a Lucky Dip, laced erratically by something between nightmare and farce. But Bailey did not forget about him. In 1973, thirty-one years after his arrival by parachute on Christmas Day of 1942 at Mihajlović's headquarters, Bailey attended a conference held in London to reconsider British policy towards wartime resistance in Yugoslavia. Discussion was scholarly, analytical and based upon a thorough trawl of official papers and personal memories.

One of Bailey's personal memories was of the sort of stuff that was rained down to him from above and had to be explained away to a growingly sceptical and irate Mihajlović. Bailey still felt strongly enough about it to suggest that even at that late date it should be investigated.

A comment by Sir Fitzroy Maclean, who commanded the British Mission to Tito and the Partisans, may have reassured Bailey that he had not been the sole victim of a private vendetta conducted by a deranged practical joker.

Maclean's Mission, it seemed, had once been sent a whole lot of detonators, volatile things capable of exploding if not carefully handled, enclosed loose with their mail.

INFLATED GRATITUDE

AFTER the successful completion in the autumn of 1944 of prolonged operations on the Albanian coast, a force consisting of No. 2 Commando, No. 40 Royal Marine Commando, and supporting artillery, set its sights thankfully on its next objective, the island of Corfu.

The Albanian imbroglio had been characterized by painful and exhausting movement over razor-sharp rocks, acrimonious collaboration with rapacious local allies more ambitious to loot the stores of their liberators than to fight their oppressors, and a turn for the worse in the weather that engendered two hundred casualties from exposure and from trench feet. Corfu, it was felt, might offer something better. It was unlikely to be able to devise much worse.

On the evening before the troops embarked in their landing craft the RAF reported that white flags were on prominent display around the island's main harbour. The Germans had gone. An advance party of the brigade commander and a few of his staff went ahead in a motor launch.

Their welcome was encouraging to the point of embarrassment. They were greeted by uninhibited applause, kisses, bouquets of flowers and an emotional speech by the archbishop. The brigadier and his followers, scratching at Albanian lice and one of them with a leg of his trousers missing, were described in this address as not human. They were demi-Gods, angels sent by God to bring peace and restore freedom. The verminous advanced guard of the heavenly host sat through these satisfying tributes looking modestly at their fingernails, and the brigadier replied becomingly. The angels then bent their minds to practical matters.

The administrative support from Italy for the expedition had all along been inadequate. Supplies would have to be supplemented by local purchase. Since none of the brigade party had any money, let alone Greek money, the half-trousered half-god was sent to negotiate a loan from the local bank manager.

The bank manager, inspired by the general enthusiasm and elevated by the archbishop's oratory, was as cooperative as could be. He opened his strongroom and assembled a huge stack of notes, neatly subdivided into bundles held together by rubber bands. He counted these carefully, prepared a receipt and passed it over for signature. The emissary found himself committing His Majesty's Government, in a transaction of which they had no knowledge, to the later reimbursement of two thousand five hundred million drachmae.

He felt no inclination to argue about the extent of this largesse. He did think it prudent to ask about its sterling equivalent. It was after all in his name, and the Treasury would catch up with him sooner or later.

The bank manager said that for obvious reasons dealings in foreign exchange had been in abeyance during the past four years. He could calculate only an approximate figure, but he could guarantee that it would be more or less accurate. He sat at his desk, did some elaborate arithmetic and rechecked it, watched throughout with resigned interest by the recipient.

'Six pounds, six shillings,' said the bank manager at last.

POST-BATTLE CUSTOMS

ROMAN legions returning from a successful campaign were greeted by a Triumph, with laurel wreaths for the boss, a parade through the streets of the capital with captured slaves in chains clanking among the victors and mass popular adulation.

Napoleon's soldiers in parallel circumstances got something similar, less the slaves, but with compensatory attentions after the ceremonies from patriotic ladies and a distribution of unlimited wine at no cost to the consumer.

In more recent times in the United States the Boys who came back when It was Over Over There did fairly well too. They marched through New York in a column about twenty men wide, whilst grateful crowds roared plaudits and the clerical staff in high-rise office blocks, having shredded redundant copies of correspondence and old telephone directories, showered down the product in a snowstorm of confetti.

Matters were conducted differently for the Glider Pilot Regiment at Down Ampney.

It was to Down Ampney, a more than usually rural air base in the South of England, that some of the survivors of the regiment were delivered after they had made their contribution to the 6th Airborne Division's drop in March 1945, during the Rhine crossing. The pilots, flying vulnerable Horsas and Hamilcars towed by powered aircraft to above the landing zone and then released, had had a wearying few days. Four hundred and forty gliders had set out from England. Thirty-five suffered broken tow-ropes and had to come down where and how they could. Two ditched in the sea. When the balance reached the Rhine near Wesel, a combination of the smokescreen established to cover the riverborne assault and a great pall of dust from the effects of the support bombing and shelling obscured the landing zone.

German anti-aircraft fire was intense, and because the ponderous manoeuvrings of slow-moving gliders preparing to land provided easy targets, effective. Ten gliders were shot down, three hundred were damaged, and most of the last had casualties aboard when they reached earth. Thirty-five more were destroyed on the ground by gunfire before they could be unloaded.

From the undamaged, and partially damaged, ones, the pilots, still being shot at extensively, supervised the despatch of the guns, vehicles, and bulldozers that they had carried with them to sustain the lightly armed parachute troops who had dropped earlier. Then the pilots began the second part of their role: to fight on the ground as trained infantry. The battle lasted for less than twenty-four hours. By the time that it was finished the Glider Pilots had had 38 per cent casualties.

The group flown home to Down Ampney was welcomed by a man clasping a clipboard and dressed in a blue uniform.

'Good afternoon,' he said courteously, 'anything to declare? I'm from HM Customs and Excise. If you'll each take one of these forms and list on it any dutiable gifts and purchases that you've made while you were abroad . . .'

A LADY'S HONOUR

IN August 1945, members of the Malayan Country Section of Force 136, the Far Eastern wing of Special Operations Executive, were faced at short notice with a task entirely different from the one for which they had trained and prepared themselves.

They had parachuted into Japanese-held Malaya in widely separated small missions to liaise with, supply and train the guerrillas of a Communist-led organization, the Malayan Peoples' Anti-Japanese Army. The MPAJA were a surly and devious lot, partners in an alliance of temporary convenience to both parties, whose agreed role was to harass and disrupt Japanese rear communications after a major seaborne landing of British and Indian troops on the peninsula.

The dropping of the atomic bombs on Hiroshima and Nagasaki, and the consequential Japanese surrender, pre-empted the assault landing, Operation Zipper, in its originally planned form and led to its substitution by something less aggressive. This in turn was delayed by high level Anglo–American bickering about who should occupy where in Asia and when, much of this argument being engendered by the determination of General Douglas MacArthur to stage a sort of showbiz surrender ceremony in Tokyo before any publicity thunder was stolen by lesser extravaganzas elsewhere.

The result was a delay before main force British troops reached Malaya. The MPAJA, whose long-term objective was a Communist takeover, left their jungle bases, moved into as many towns and villages as they could get at, proclaimed that they had defeated the Japanese single-handed and began to shed the blood of old political opponents.

The Force 136 teams, whose preoccupations until a few days before had been with ambush tactics, demolition charges and similar, found themselves trying to save lives, wrangling with their old cooperators and doing what they could to preserve public order. In default of anybody else to do the job they also took on responsibility for local administration.

One of these *de facto* governors of a badly run-down, exhausted country was a former rubber planter named Gregory. Captain Gregory was a man of much commonsense who spoke Malay and Tamil. By means of a policy compounded of bluff and vigorous intervention he managed to keep Communist excesses more or less, but not entirely, under some sort of control. When he could take time off from that, he bent his energies to the restoration of communications, the movement of food supplies, the settlement of disputes and all manner of other things in which, as he cheerfully admitted, he was inexperienced. Like most of his colleagues in other districts, he hoped to God repeatedly that the main force would hurry up and arrive so that he could hand over his new responsibilities to those who were professionally fitted to discharge them.

His particular fief was a remote district on the east coast. For the mobilization of labour to do the many things that had to be done he was dependent upon the goodwill of the local community leaders. He was patiently, scrupulously tactful with them. He found it difficult. No flashes of warm sympathy bound him to Che Yusuf, Mr Yap, and Mr Ramalingam. There were two reasons for this. The first was that each of them was publicly genial to each of the others, but would then come privately to Gregory to tell him how unreliable, half-witted, dishonest and self-seeking their fellow leaders were. The second was that when neither of the other two was present the one who was insisted upon recommending himself for the OBE.

They seemed to be obsessed with the OBE. They supplied him individually with dubious evidence of their heroic resistance to the Japanese occupiers, and piled upon it

'I shan't need you this evening, Tomkins.'

spurious claims of their achievements in restoring the district to post-hostilities normality. They knew much more about the mechanics of the compilation of the honours list than Gregory did. 'Too late now for the King's birthday list,' said Che

Yusuf, Mr Yap and Mr Ramalingam, singly and confidentially, 'but if you get my recommendation in quick it should be
OK for the New Year's Honours.'

Gregory stayed blandly non-committal and kept his
temper. At times, when the pressure of self-recommendation
became more than usually insistent, he wondered wistfully if
there were a sort of reverse Honours List, held by the College
of Heralds or whoever looked after these matters, consisting of
nominations of people who in no circumstances should ever be
awarded the OBE. If so, he had his part of the team picked.

After a frustrating day that had been particularly thick with
covert inter-communal recrimination and proffered supple-
mentary material to be added to citations, Gregory made his
way back irritably to the rest house. On the current Gregory
scale-of-appreciation-of-comparative-worth the rest house
and Tan (its cook, manager and overall operator) got top
marks. If only everyone in the district, specifically the
community leaders, would manage their affairs as competently and unfussily as Tan managed his, considered Gregory,
life would be infinitely sweeter.

When Gregory and his signaller had first walked into the
town from the jungle, the rest house had looked as dilapidated
as was everything else after three and a half years of Japanese
occupation. White ants had ravaged many of the wooden slats
of the walls. Other slats had been wrenched loose as had
several lengths of the verandah railing, presumably during
some Japanese drunken festivity. The whole place was filthy.
The garden was riotously overgrown. For want of anywhere
better, Gregory had set up his headquarters amidst the
squalor. Tan arrived the same afternoon and asked diffidently
if he could have his old job back. Gregory said Yes, on
probation.

It was a good decision. Tan and his wife, a small, rather
intimidating woman with a determined expression, began by
cleaning and refurbishing one of the bedrooms for Gregory.
They brought the kitchen back into use. Over a period of days
they scrubbed the inside of the building from top to bottom,
cut the grass and dug and planted flower beds. Tan pruned the

bougainvillaca that straggled up one of the uprights of the verandah. He showed an unexpected aptitude at plumbing and carpentry. He restored the water supply. He mended furniture, replaced the damaged and the more conspicuously ant-ridden slats and put the verandah railing together again.

These preliminaries completed, Tan and his wife maintained standards. Inside and out, all was clean and tidy. Both Tan and his wife were cooks of rare talent, launderers of skill and devotees of hard work.

On this hot late afternoon Gregory climbed the steps of the verandah, and threw his beret and his pistol on to a bamboo chair. Tan at once appeared with a glass of iced lime juice and a plate of fruit. He also brought a message that had been delivered by Gregory's signaller, now established in residence at the police station, where reception for his set was better and the telephone occasionally worked.

The message was an *en clair* signal from Force 136 headquarters in Ceylon. British troops had disembarked in force at Morib on the west coast. Advanced elements should reach Gregory's district on the following morning. With them would be Colonel Rogers, late of the Malayan civil service, now with the newly formed military administration. Rogers would take over responsibility for civil affairs on arrival. The message ended on a note that left Gregory wondering whether the sender was being pompous or jocular: 'Thank you for all that you have done in the discharge of your duties as one of His Majesty's representatives.'

It was news to Gregory that he had been – and for a few hours more still was – one of His Majesty's representatives. There was a satisfying high-falutin ring to the title, but his pleasure in it was outweighed by a deeper solace. Somebody else, properly qualified, would now inherit the task of trying to get some sense out of those contentious leaders of their peoples, Che Yusaf, Mr Yap and Mr Ramalingam. He was glad that this unhappy mantle was about to fall upon Rogers, whom he knew of old. Rogers was an unbending, self-important do-gooder, a stickler for bureaucratic proprieties, a rank-conscious temporary soldier who had turned himself into an imitation martinet. The Yusuf–Yap–Ramalingam combination should give him something to think about. Rogers would doubtless make himself as unpleasant as possible during Gregory's handover to him, but if Gregory had anything to do with it it would go down in the record book for the brevity with which it was conducted and the speed at which he got the hell out.

Gregory supposed that he should tell Che Yusuf and Messrs Yap and Ramalingam that formal liberation was at least imminent, and that the capricious threat to life and limb from trigger-happy Communist guerrillas was about to be lifted. He baulked at the thought. He had had more than enough of them for one day. They could wait till the morning. But he himself felt an urge towards celebration. There was no one to celebrate with and, even if there had been, no suitable stimulants to celebrate with either.

However, immediately to hand there was somebody, the most deserving case of all, in whom to confide. Simply, and with a quiet sense of satisfaction, Gregory told Tan of what was due to happen on the morrow.

Tan looked delighted. He said that he *was* delighted. He went to tell Mrs Tan. There was a lot of excited chatter in the kitchen. Tan returned conspiratorially and said that in honour of the occasion two things were about to happen. The first was that Mrs Tan would cook a special Chinese *makan* for Gregory. The second was a surprise.

Tan went off to develop his surprise. There was the sound of digging from a corner of the garden. This was followed by a further raucous dialogue in the kitchen, a lot of clattering about and the reappearance of Tan dressed in a spotless white tunic with a high collar and bearing a tray. On the tray was a bottle of whisky, a full ice-bucket, a jug of water and a tumbler.

Gregory stared at the bottle. He had last seen whisky six months previously, on the night in Ceylon before he was parachuted into Malaya. Where had this come from? Tan explained, beaming. Three and a half years ago, he said, when word had come that the Japanese were advancing fast from Kuantan, Tan had buried a case of scotch in the rest house garden. With it he had placed a sword, left behind in a room by a British officer who had gone in a hurry with the rest of the British soldiers. Tan had thought of uncovering his cache earlier, but had decided against it. He didn't want his treasure to fall into the hands of those barbarous Communist bandits who kept threatening him subtly when the tuan was not present. That danger was now nearly past. Tan spooned some ice into the tumbler, added a measure of whisky, topped it up with water and handed it to Gregory.

'*Stengah whisky ayer, tuan,*' he said happily.

Gregory looked admiringly at Tan, raised his glass to him, drank and suggested that Tan should have a tot himself. Tan declined courteously. He didn't drink on duty he said. Later perhaps. In the meantime let Gregory go ahead by himself.

Gregory did. He had three reflective slugs before dinner. Then he showered and changed and came to the table. Tan had laid out chopsticks, and lots of little bowls with delicate sauces in them and then brought a succession of delights from Mrs Tan, the flavour of each complementing the last. Tan apologized for the lack of wine or beer and poured more whisky instead. Gregory ate mightily and toasted Tan frequently. Mrs Tan, in the kitchen, became increasingly noisy whenever Tan went to collect something new from her. Gregory assumed that she did not share Tan's reservations about drinking on duty and that she had broached one of the other bottles from Tan's buried case. Whatever the cause, Gregory felt mildly disturbed about disharmony in the Tan union, sympathetic at this surprise revelation that even this superb character Tan had his Achilles' heel, a wife who on occasion browbeat him.

After the last course Gregory went to the kitchen and made a small speech of thanks to Mrs Tan. Then he sat contentedly on the verandah. Tan again brought out the tray with the scotch and the ice, and this time produced for inspection the unearthed sword. There were traces of mud on the scabbard, but otherwise it was in perfect condition. Tan had greased the blade and the hilt carefully before burying it. Gregory put the sword on the table and fixed his gaze upon it, pondering yet again on the excellence of Tan.

Thoughts of the excellence of Tan, and of its converse, the absence of excellence in Che Yusaf, Mr Yap and Mr Ramalingam with their interminable self-promotion for their OBEs, mingled a bit mistily with the notion that he might as well drink a toast to himself in his last hours as one of His Majesty's Representatives. This drink in turn led to further contemplation of the sword, and then everything came together in his mind. He rose to his feet, picked up the sword by its hilt, and roared, 'Tan!'

Tan hurried out from the kitchen.

'Kneel down,' said Gregory, briskly.

Tan, with recent memories of what had happened in the district to people instructed to kneel down by Japanese officers brandishing swords, took his time over it. Finally Gregory, in a courtly manner, put his mind at rest. Tan knelt.

Gregory tapped him lightly on both shoulders with the point of the sword.

'Arise, Sir Tan,' he said solemnly. 'On behalf of His Majesty King George the Sixth, I declare you to be a Knight of the Most Excellent Order of the British Empire.'

And that, thought Gregory to himself, was true justice. A fair crack of the whip for someone who really deserved recognition, and one each in the eye for Che Yusuf, Mr Yap, and Mr Ramalingam.

Sir Tan arose. He accepted the offer of a celebratory drink. He went to tell his wife of what had happened. A further bonus was evident there. All animosity faded from her voice. Gregory reached for a word to describe her tone, and found it. Cooed was what she'd done. He poured another drink to mark this pleasing piece of marital reconciliation, and after that he didn't remember very much except for the care with which he wrote out and signed a temporary certificate in which was enshrined Tan's new status.

Gregory awoke under his mosquito net feeling awful. Tan was placing a tray with a glass of chilled lime juice and a plate of small bananas on a low table. Birds were singing outside.

Tan had news. There was high excitement in the town. A small convoy of British army vehicles had reached the outskirts. Gregory swung his legs off the bed, gulped the lime juice, and thought dully that he'd better move fast if he were to be in time to greet appropriately that pompous functionary with the rat-trap mouth, Colonel Rogers.

He was staring critically into the shaving mirror at his bloodshot eyes when the events of the previous evening began to come back to him. Christ. The knighting of Tan. The kneeling, and the taps with the sword. Worse, that bloody scroll or manifesto or whatever its right name was, with all that florid, contrived Heralds' language about letting all present know that the trusty and well-beloved Tan had been invested by His Majesty's representative, Thomas Harry Gregory, Captain in the General Service Corps, with the office and dignity of a Knight of the Most Excellent Order of the British Empire. If Rogers ever saw that . . .

'Tan,' bawled Gregory.

Tan arrived smoothly and said: 'Tuan?'

'That business last night,' said Gregory, 'It was all a mistake. I'd had too much to drink.'

'I see,' said Tan, after a pause.

'Where's that paper I wrote out?'

'Hanging over the sideboard in the dining room. I framed it early this morning.'

'Well, for Christ's sake take it down and give it back to me. Your knighthood's revoked.'

Tan looked at him steadily, understandingly and adamantly.

'It's not as easy as that, sir,' he said. '*I* fully appreciate the position. *I'm* prepared to accept that it shouldn't have happened and to forget about it. The problem is that Lady Tan certainly won't. She's already gone to tell Che Yusuf's wife, and Mrs Yap, and Mrs Ramalingam.'

'My God, Tan. Get her back.'

'Too late, sir. She left over an hour . . .'

From outside came the growing sound of engines, of vehicle wheels on the drive, of vehicles stopping. There were footsteps on the verandah.

'Where's Captain Gregory?' called a precise, irritable voice. 'I was expecting him to meet me. My name's Rogers, Colonel Rogers.'

LANTERNS ARE FOR THE BIRDS

'SOMERVILLE,' said the district officer, economically limning a character sketch, 'is a very brave man, a narrow-minded, old-fashioned snob, and a bachelor with the domestic habits of a fussy Victorian spinster. He's also the chairman of the District Planters' Association and has a lot of pull in Kuala Lumpur.'

'I see,' said the colonel.

'Also, he keeps a parrot,' said the district officer. 'Bloody nuisance, the parrot. Interrupts conversations.'

'I see,' said the colonel again.

'What I'm getting round to in a heavy-footed sort of way is that although it's not for a civilian like me to try to influence the details of how you dispose of your battalion, it would do no harm to the District War Committee if the subaltern you put on Somerville's estate were to be something of a social whizz-kid. The sort of fellow who says Sir from time to time, and doesn't spit in his soup to cool it.'

'How did you like East Africa, old man?'

'Thanks for the advice,' said the colonel. 'And thanks for the drink.' He stood up to leave. The district officer saw him to his Land Rover.

'I'll send Lloyd,' said the colonel before he climbed aboard. 'He went to Eton, and washes regularly.'

The platoon base on Sungei Ular Estate had previously been the assistant manager's bungalow, a low building of weathered roof tiles and white-painted wooden slats, sited skilfully to catch prevailing breezes. On two sides there was a raised verandah, with hibiscus planted at intervals below it and bougainvillaea trained up most of the uprights. Lloyd set himself up inside the house together with his platoon sergeant, the signaller and one of his sections. The other two sections were in tents in the garden.

Beyond the garden, on all sides, were rubber trees, acres and acres of them, growing in regimented orderliness, grey boles and dull green leaves, incised tapping panels shaped like sergeant's chevrons, creamy juice bleeding slowly into the attached earthenware latex cups. A laterite track, startlingly orange against the greens and greys of the rubber, cut through the trees to join with the network of estate roads that linked the office, the factory, the smokehouse, the labour lines and Somerville's elegant house, two hundred yards away on a low knoll.

By day it was unchangingly hot and sticky. Early mornings, evenings and nights were comfortably warm. Bulbuls and Straits robins carolled during the cool periods after dawn and before dusk. Gibbons wahwahed away beyond the jungle edge to the east.

Lloyd was wary of the nearby laterite track. Three months before, when the battalion was still at Catterick readying itself for Malaya, the bungalow's last occupant, Somerville's assistant, had died on the track, along with his escort of six Malay special constables, in a short-range ambush by Communist terrorists. As well as seven lives, seven weapons had been lost. It was that incident, and Somerville's coldly angry reaction to it, that had led to the detachment of a platoon to the estate. Fragmenting units into penny packets had little appeal to the military, but Somerville had a case and something had to be done about it.

Lloyd was a well-trained and competent young officer. He did his conscientious best to meet his defined task of 'dominating Sungei Ular Estate and its adjacent jungle, up to and including the Ular river to the east and the main north–south road to the west'. His patrols left their base unobtrusively in the dark and laid up all day, sweatily and patiently, bothered by boredom and insects, in selected ambush positions. Lloyd, in alternation with his platoon sergeant, led one section at a time in ostentatious progresses through the rubber during the morning working hours, with a view to re-establishing the confidence and morale of a badly intimidated body of tappers, weeders and Tamil and Chinese supervisors.

It was tedious hit-or-miss work, which initially went unrewarded. The bandit intimidation continued. During the first week two Chinese women tappers, operating on the southernmost field of the estate, were beaten to death for their unreceptiveness to demands for contributions of food and money to the Malayan Peoples' Liberation Army. On the Tuesday of the second week one of Somerville's latex lorries, on its way with its load towards the smokehouse, was stopped and set on fire. The Tamil driver escaped with a warning harangue about the evils and perils of collaboration with capitalist exploiters. On the Thursday night the tapping panels of an acre of rubber trees were slashed by *parangs* into unproductivity and their latex bowls were smashed. On the Friday night some ill-aimed rifle shots, fired from a distance, were put into Somerville's upstairs verandah.

Lloyd mounted follow-ups to each of these incidents. The follow-ups achieved nothing. The rubber and jungle offered too rich a cover for guerrillas who chose their own targets and timings, and who disappeared fast when they had done what they wanted to do.

Throughout this frustrating period Lloyd, obedient to exhortations from his colonel, which had been reinforced by more saltily expressed ones from his company commander, was scrupulously courteous to Somerville. Their dealings were formal. Lloyd called Somerville Sir. Somerville called Lloyd Lloyd. Somerville was cooperatively efficient in lending Lloyd large-scale maps and in showing him around the intricacies of the grounds of the estate. He was helpful with useful information about which sections of his labourers he suspected of being most under the bandits' thumbs, and which fields they worked in.

There was no warmth in these offerings. Somerville was reserved, unsmiling and withdrawn. He did not invite Lloyd to his house. Lloyd thought this last strange, but a relief. A bout of frozen hospitality from Somerville would not be an occasion of joy.

Midway through the fourth week, one of Lloyd's sections had a minor success. Its ambush position, placed fortuitously in the right place at the right time, was approached by a cautiously moving single file of bandits. The corporal became over-excited and opened fire too early, but the Bren-gunner killed the leading bandit. The rest dispersed, fast. The follow-up failed. The body of the dead man was carried in, and the carbine that he had with him was identified by Somerville as having belonged to his murdered assistant.

On the following day Somerville invited Lloyd to tea. Somerville didn't simply say, 'Drop in for tea.' He wrote a letter, delivered by his cook-boy: 'Dear Lloyd, If you are free would you care to join me for tea at 4 p.m. today, 20th November 1951? Yours sincerely, G. B. Somerville.'

Lloyd, constricted by his orders, exasperated by the waste of time both of the tea and of the archaic formalities, replied with a letter sent by hand of a runner: 'Dear Mr Somerville, Thank you for your kind invitation to tea at 4 p.m. today, 20th November 1951. I accept with great pleasure. Yours sincerely, D. P. Lloyd.'

He changed into a clean jungle-green uniform and walked the two hundred yards along the path through the rubber to Somerville's house. It was an immaculately maintained establishment of polished hardwood floors, Persian rugs, gleaming silver trophies, bamboo furniture with flowered chintz cushion covers, framed water-colours and sibilant ceiling fans. There was tea and seed cake and bone china and polite small talk. Much attention was given to Somerville's parrot, an ill-mannered and truculent bird that fluttered about in a small cage and squawked incessantly. Somerville affectionately interpreted its chatter for Lloyd, and fed it crumbs of seed cake, and cooed at it. Lloyd endured all this with distinction. He left with well-bred words of gratitude and a hope that Somerville wouldn't be hospitable too often.

An operational lull followed the infliction of the first bandit casualty. The bandits had had things their way for a very long time and were unused to setbacks. Lloyd continued to place his ambushes and lead his patrols, but overt bandit activity fell away. Part of their problem was getting adequate food. Chinese squatters, once a fertile source of bandit supply, had by now nearly all been resettled in wired and defended villages. Outlying estate labourers had been regrouped into fenced labour lines, guarded by Malay special constables. A little rice could be smuggled through the checkpoints by dedicated or terrorized Communist supporters, but it did not meet bandit requirements. Sooner or later they would have to chance major attempts to lift food.

Lloyd was summoned to battalion headquarters to be told of a planned attempt. His company commander took him to see Inspector Tan at the district police headquarters. Tan was an expressionless young Chinese special branch officer who by use of a sophisticated mixture of applied psychology and the straightforward trading of cash for knowledge, manipulated a shifting and shifty cast of informers. His latest acquisition needed neither psychological pressure nor money. His motive was vengeance. He had been the husband of one of the two women beaten to death during Lloyd's first week on Sungei Ular Estate. He had high-grade hot news.

The *Min Yuen*, the Communist back-up organization, was assembling a quantity of food, mostly rice but including rolled oats, Bovril and similar nourishing items, within one of the blocks in Somerville's labour lines. The food was being divided into easily carried loads packed in sacking. The sacks were put into a pig-sty abutting the perimeter fence at a place where bumpy ground made it relatively easy for intruders to crawl under the bottom strands of wire undetected by the special constabulary guards.

A bandit foodlift party was due to come to the wire to collect supplies after midnight on the following Saturday. The informer was explicit about the details. He had been impressed as a helper by the *Min Yuen* who held to the misguided belief that what they had done to his wife would have taught him his lesson and that he could now be relied upon to cooperate with them.

Lloyd's preparations were skilful and thorough. To go to examine the ground around the pig-sty and the adjacent fence would induce suspicious nervousness among the *Min Yuen*. Lloyd found a climbable tree up which he could go unnoticed and study the area through binoculars. His solution to the problem posed was the product of much thought, detailed briefing, three rehearsals in a remote part of the estate and, after dusk on the Saturday night, delicately conducted, silent movement by night.

His patrol was hidden, alert and in position when the foodlift party was first sensed, then heard, then seen in the tropical starlight. Lloyd didn't hurry things. He waited until the transfer of sacks was well under way before opening up with his Sterling. His first burst was the signal for the others to fire, for flares to be put up. The flares gave a comprehensive, sharply defined illumination to the scene, accentuating the edges between splashed light and dark shadow. There were a few lethal, concentrated seconds of noise and confusion. Lloyd roared, 'Stop!' The shooting stopped. Five bandit bodies lay among the scattering of punctured sacks with rice dribbling from them. Blood trails showed that at least two other bandits had been wounded.

Lloyd, who had shot two himself, and who had not before killed a human, felt slightly sickened. He did not show it. He had a busy night and succeeding day.

He mounted a follow-up, fruitless as usual, in pursuit of the surviving bandits. He reported by radio to battalion headquarters. Before dawn the officer in charge of the police district drove out with Inspector Tan. The OCPD saw Somerville, imposed an extended curfew upon the labour lines, and with the aid of special branch detectives arrested a carefully chosen range of suspects from the *Min Yuen* cell, the selection having been made in a manner that did not compromise the informer. Tan checked the bodies against the 'wanted' list and identified all but one.

The district officer and the colonel arrived at nine o'clock. The district officer spoke to Somerville, and then addressed a muster of the labour force. For the first time on this estate since the Emergency began in 1948, he said, the people who had been intimidating and extorting and murdering had been hit where it hurt. With more public cooperation the menace could be removed altogether, and the country could move ahead to the democratic election of an indigenous government to take over peacefully after the planned independence.

The colonel cast a professional eye over the site of the little action, questioned Lloyd, congratulated him and went to thank the troops. By the time the visitors had all gone away and Lloyd had tidied things up, arranged that night's patrolling programme and attended to necessary administrative chores, it was four o'clock in the afternoon. He had had an emotionally and physically exhausting night, a busy day and no sleep. He handed over to his platoon sergeant and said that he was to be disturbed only in exceptional circumstances. He climbed wearily under his mosquito net and slept deeply.

At 6.30 he was shaken awake by one of the sentries, bearing an envelope marked 'Immediate'. It had been delivered by Somerville's cook, who was waiting to take back the reply. Lloyd opened the envelope sleepily. Dear Lloyd, if he were free, was invited to dinner. Dress informal. 7 for 7.30. Dear Lloyd, who had been hoping for about twelve hours of uninterrupted unconsciousness, thanked Dear Mr Somerville for his kind invitation and accepted with pleasure.

Lloyd showered, dressed himself in civilian shirt, tie and slacks, and had a mug of tea. He looked outside. It was an overcast evening. The moon would rise later, but at this time the path through the rubber to Somerville's house would be in total darkness. He would need a torch to help him over eroded patches and potholes, and to identify himself to the special constabulary guards who manned a raised concrete *kubu* behind the barbed wire that surrounded Somerville's garden. The SCs had cause to be trigger-happy.

Lloyd was annoyed to find that the battery of his own torch was running flat. The signaller had one, but he needed it in case the estate generator failed or was sabotaged. The platoon sergeant could not be parted from his for the same reason. The signaller had an idea. Among the undisturbed impedimenta left behind in the bungalow by the dead assistant planter was an old storm lantern. They checked the kerosene level, turned up the wick, and lit it. It was in good working condition.

Somerville, his reserve modified, rose smilingly to greet Lloyd. Somerville looked at the lantern and said that he was glad to see that that old thing was still in use. It had once belonged to him when he was a young assistant, nearly thirty years earlier. It had been handed down the generations. Good workmanship always prevailed. He took it, turned down the wick, and put it on the bookcase beside the parrot's cage. The parrot became cantankerous, Somerville soothed it with old-maidish clucking noises.

The cook hovered. Somerville asked Lloyd what he would drink. Lloyd said orange juice. Somerville said engagingly that he had no intention of forcing strong drink upon anyone who didn't want it, but after all Lloyd had something to celebrate. He had helped to lift a great load of fear from a great many people of all races. It was not every day that the bandits got their comeuppance as thoroughly as Lloyd had given it to them. Why not try a *stengah* whisky soda? Lloyd did.

He had two. Usually he drank very little. At the dinner table, aglitter with glass and silver on polished wood, with an arrangement of pink hibiscus as a centrepiece, the cook served chilled Chablis with thefish and Bordeaux with the meat. Lloyd's glass kept getting refilled. Lloyd became very talkative. He told Somerville that the cook was a master-cook and that Somerville was a brilliant conversationalist. After a delicious, blurred confection of meringue and ice-cream, they went back to the chintz and bamboo chairs for further fascinating talk, coffee and brandy. Lloyd remembered laughing happily at some scintillating witticism of Somerville's, and he remembered accepting a second glass of brandy, and after that he remembered nothing at all.

He awoke, stiff and uncomfortable, in the armchair that he had been sitting in earlier. All the lights were on. Somerville had gone. The house was silent. Lloyd looked at his watch. It was 4.10 a.m.

An envelope addressed to him was propped against a glass on the occasional table to his front. He opened the envelope.

'Dear Lloyd,' the letter read, 'You fell asleep. Normally, I have little time for guests who drink more than they can hold and make fools of themselves. In this instance I hold myself entirely to blame.

'On Saturday you did a splendid night's work. It was followed by a hard day. What you needed then was a splendid night's sleep. You were courteous enough to accept, at short notice, my invitation to dine. If I had been more thoughtful and less impetuous I would have deferred it until you had had the chance of a decent rest. I know how you must have felt. I felt much the same at your age, when in different conditions but with similar strains, I did more or less the same as you did, in my case in the Ypres salient in 1917.

'I suggest that you go home to bed and, if you are free, come round for a recuperative glass of beer at 12 noon tomorrow. Or, if you prefer it, a recuperative glass of orange juice. Yours sincerely, G. B. Somerville.'

Lloyd felt relief and thankfulness. He stood up, stretched, picked up his lantern from the bookcase and went out into the garden. The moon had risen, the cloud abated. There was no need to light the lantern. The special constables bade him goodnight. Five minutes later he was in his camp bed under the mosquito net, thinking, before he dropped into a deep sleep, that old Somerville, cold, prickly, pernickety old Somerville, wasn't such a bad old buffer after all.

The signaller awakened him by shaking him by the shoulder. Lloyd looked at his watch. It was a quarter to seven in the morning.

'That planter's cook, sir,' said the signaller, 'he's brought another letter. Says it's urgent.' It was.

'Dear Lloyd, My cook is returning your lantern. Will you please give him back my parrot? I think that it would be as well if you did *not* come round for a drink today at 12 noon. Yours sincerely, G. B. Somerville.'

THE SHARP END OF DINNER

THE Imperial Defence College, in recent years renamed the Royal College of Defence Studies, was, and under its new title is, an institution for the higher education of senior officers of all three services. Selected students of the rank of brigadier and its equivalents, all picked for promotion to higher things, some to the highest things, assemble for a year of study, tuition and discussion. There is a sophisticated curriculum. Emphasis is upon strategic higher thinking, but much time is devoted to the interplay between military strategy and international politics and economics. Aside from the domestic British military intake, chosen nominees come to the course from the diplomatic and home civil services and from some Commonwealth countries.

A valuable feature of the course is the overseas tour. Syndicates of fifteen or so students, each syndicate accompanied by a member of the directing staff, visit differing parts of the world, North America say, or Southeast Asia, or the Central Mediterranean. They are usually received hospitably (countries on each itinerary are selected with care), briefed conscientiously and guided extensively around the military, industrial and development establishments and projects of their hosts.

One of these syndicates, on the Mediterranean beat in the 1960s, made its way to Crete. Crete had little of industrial or development interest to put on display, but it was a beautiful island with a recent past of unusual military interest. The Germans had taken it in 1941 from its British, New Zealand and Australian defenders in an airborne operation so expensive in casualties to the assault force that the Germans never again used their parachute troops as parachute troops. From Crete onwards German parachutists fought in an infantry role.

Complementary matters for consideration by the students were the part played by the Royal Navy in first sustaining the garrison and then, with a heavy loss of lives and ships, evacuating such of the soldiers as could be got away; and the overwhelming effectiveness with which the *Luftwaffe* had dominated the skies during the battle.

The syndicate was taken to see Maleme, Heraklion and other sites of bygone strife. They took notes, studied maps, asked questions and exchanged views. On the last night of their visit they were invited to dinner by a Greek general.

Among the general's other guests was one chosen specially for the occasion. His name was Markos, and he had an outstanding record as a guerrilla leader. After the evacuation of the British force he had taken to the hills, from which he harried and ambushed the German occupiers, succoured British troops left behind on the island and still evading capture, and cooperated fearlessly with parties from the Special Boat Section and from Special Operations Executive who came to Crete by submarine or parachute or *caique* to gather intelligence and to attack German aircraft on the ground. The general barely knew Markos, who now lived in a remote mountain village, but he knew all about his formidable reputation.

The general was a polished and urbane host. The dinner table, glistening with silver and crystal laid on a long damask cloth, stood under a vine-bedecked trellis on a stone terrace overlooking the sea. Above it was a velvet sky, bright with stars and a silvery half-moon. The food was superb, the wine good and plentiful. The British guests thought the setting enchanting and the hospitality delightful.

There was, however, a minor incongruity amongst these smooth proceedings. It early became clear that Markos's distinguished gifts as a guerrilla fighter were unmatched by familiarity with the more fancy niceties of behaviour at a dinner party. He lacked what at the time were customarily known as Representational Qualifications. A tall, thickly bearded burly man, he seemed to be partially drunk when he arrived, a condition that generated in him a paranoid moroseness rather than merriment.

He knew no English. He spoke in a Cretan dialect so impenetrable that even the general and his staff had difficulty in working out what he was talking about, which was perhaps just as well because most of it seemed to be either offensive or complaining.

Markos became drunker and drunker. As he did so, his savage gloom increased and his table manners further deteriorated. He ate his food with his fingers, belched thunderously when he felt like it and glared in silent malevolence at the British brigadier seated opposite him.

The Greek general became increasingly uneasy and then irritated. Markos was in danger of destroying a pleasant and useful evening's entertainment. He had been included in the guest list on advice from Athens; the general was beginning to wish that he hadn't taken the advice. Markos, still pouring wine down his gullet as if there were no tomorrow, was by now beginning to broaden the scope of the recipients included in his horrible scowl. He was shifting it at evenly spaced intervals around the table, staring threateningly at each of the intellectual cream of the British and Commonwealth armed forces. The general admired the unworried aplomb with which they responded.

A further thought crossed the general's mind. He began to wonder if Markos was so far gone in wine and confusion that in his mental fog he had lost sight of who these guests were. Had he subconsciously drifted back to wartime, convinced that he was surrounded by *German* officers, was on the edge of betrayal at some Germanic military equivalent of the Last Supper?

The general's patience finally broke when the roast suckling pig arrived. Waiters brought the big silver dishes around the table to each guest in turn. All but one helped themselves dexterously with the serving implements provided. When it came to Markos's turn he wiped his already greasy fingers on his beard, seized a large chunk of pig in his huge hands, and began to chomp it messily between his teeth.

The general's patience finally broke when the roast sucking pig arrived. Waiters brought the big silver dishes around the going to be allowed to bring shame upon the general's reputation for hospitality by continuing with this sort of uncouthness.

'*Markos,*' hissed the general. 'Knife!'

Markos dropped his piece of pig on the floor, grabbed the carving knife from the serving dish, sprang on to the table with a crash of breaking glass and china, and stood in a low, swaying crouch, the knife raised, his eyes flashing from each student of the Imperial Defence College syndicate to the next.

'Which one?' he roared to the general.

HALO SOLDIER

THE possibility that he might be remembered by posterity as the first holder of his job to have had a canonized saint under command was a source of warm satisfaction to the chaplain general. As an ordained priest of the Church of England he had no machinery at his disposal for the nomination of saints. His organization got by with the ones that it had appropriated at the Reformation, an inheritance that had caused him theological difficulties during his youth. Had saintliness simply ceased to exist after the sixteenth century? he had wondered. Alternatively, if the Catholic practice of continuing to name new saints was as suspect as he had been led to believe, should not the old list have been deleted from the official record? It had been a measure of the complexity of his doubts that when the Vatican eliminated from the calendar a large number of saints with questionable credentials, the future chaplain general had felt almost personally insulted at the inclusion of St George, the patron saint of England, among the dismissed phoneys.

These reservations were now far behind him. They had never of course entered into the calculations of his colleague, Monsignor Smyth, the senior Catholic chaplain and a close friend to whom he was attached by both personal and ecumenical ties. It was Monsignor Smyth who first mentioned the idea that Father Dominic Dobbs, lately killed in a motor car accident at Catterick, might be a possible candidate for sainthood.

None who had known him had any doubts about the saintliness of Father Dobbs. To use, as the monsignor put it, one of

those succinctly helpful things, clichés, Father Dobbs had
been a legend in his lifetime. Of frail, cadaverous and almost
unsettling appearance, with piercing eyes and a gentle hint of
a smile always at his lips, he had been a man of enormous
energy and dedication. He aimed at, some would say had
achieved, personal spiritual perfection. His private life had
been one of austere self-denial and prayerful meditation. His
official life, as a brigade chaplain, brought back memories of
quietly expressed wise counsel to the troubled, of a deeply
sympathetic understanding of human weaknesses, of an
inspiring calmness and cheerfulness in adverse circumstances
and of a simple goodness, engendered by a profound faith, that
brought comfort and confidence to everyone fortunate enough
to come within the ambit of his influence.

The Royal Army Chaplains Department had down the
years been served by many outstanding clerics of all
denominations. The chaplain general agreed with Monsignor
Smyth that they neither knew personally or knew about any
who had reached the standard of pastoral effectiveness and
personal holiness set by Father Dobbs.

Just what, asked the chaplain general, was the process by
which a member of his colleague's religion was given official
recognition of sanctity? Monsignor Smyth said that he'd never
done one before, but he was familiar with the outlines. A senior
priest of the candidate's diocese was delegated to assemble a
comprehensive dossier about his entire life. Since, in the
territorial sense, Father Dobbs had belonged to no diocese the
duty would devolve upon the monsignor himself. When the
dossier was completed it would be submitted to another
nominated senior priest, who in the role of Devil's advocate
would attempt to identify weaknesses in the case as presented.
Scrupulous care was taken to ensure that canonization was
not achieved merely as a consequence of overenthusiastic
advocacy. The responsibility of the Devil's advocate was to
temper impartiality with scepticism. If any doubts prevailed,
the recommendation would fail. A particularly close scrutiny
was applied·to the evidence submitted about the three
necessary miracles.

The Protestant susceptibilities of the chaplain general were a bit thrown by this casual talk of miracles. What miracles? he asked cautiously. The monsignor was matter-of-factly Catholic in his reply. The best definition of a miracle that he could offer, he said, came from the catechism in vogue when he was a boy. A miracle was a truth beyond reason, but revealed by God. To qualify for canonization a candidate's case must be supported by three authenticated miracles. The monsignor would arrange for appeals for information to be announced at every Mass celebrated by Catholic chaplains throughout the army.

The monsignor did so. The response was extensive, but in terms of what was being sought, disappointing. There was an impressive spread of submissions that illustrated that Father Dobbs's self-mortification and known acts of goodness had been supplemented unobtrusively by a much longer catalogue of the transmission of solace and practical kindliness than had been suspected, but the sum of the depositions, while substantiating saintliness, did nothing to demonstrate the miraculous. The monsignor reported upon this reverse to the chaplain general, who became wistful as the chances diminished of his being able to use throwaway lines like, 'That's what my friend Saint Dominic Dobbs often said to me.'

Monsignor Smyth was on the verge of abandoning hope when a letter arrived one day for him from a sergeant in an infantry battalion. The sergeant opened uncompromisingly by stating that he was himself an atheist. He had, however, overheard talk in the sergeants' mess among some of his Catholic colleagues about the search for evidence of miracles performed by Father Dobbs. Because of his own lack of belief he was reluctant to intervene, and he feared that if he did so publicly he might find himself the butt of a certain amount of derision. But Father Dobbs had been the finest man whom he had ever known. He, the sergeant, felt that he owed it to the padre's memory to place it on record that he had been present at a miracle performed by the Father. It had been after Protestant rioting in the Shankill area of Belfast. Could he come to talk in private to the monsignor about it?

Monsignor Smyth arranged a meeting for three days later. The sergeant, a smart, stocky, leathery-looking man, saluted with a faint air of embarrassment. The monsignor gave him a cup of tea, put him at his ease with some inconsequential chit-chat and came to the point. What had happened on the Shankill road?

What had happened, said the sergeant, was that after about three successive nights of uproar, with petrol bombs and rocks thrown from behind overturned hijacked cars, with casualties both to the rioters and to the army and the Royal Ulster Constabulary, and with several buildings incinerated, an exhausted, uneasy calm had fallen upon the area. The soldiers had been ordered to take all precautions to contain further violence but to avoid provocation by too ostentatious a presence. For the most part they kept their heads down. Towards the end of an edgy but peaceful morning, Father Dobbs arrived in a Land Rover at the corner of a street littered with the debris of the clashes of the previous three nights. As was his custom, the soldiers drew strength from his being with them.

All would probably have ended with his getting back into his vehicle and continuing on his rounds, had not a small girl wandered into sight at the far end of the street into which the troops had been told not to go. The child, who looked about seven, was dirty, distressed and had an improvised bandage, deeply stained with dried blood, tied around her head. Father Dobbs at once said that he was going to her to comfort her.

The sergeant tried to dissuade him. Father Dobbs was wearing a clerical collar, but he also had on a camouflaged combat jacket, combat boots and a beret with his cap badge on it. Any appearance by him in the contentious street would be likely to stir things up again. Father Dobbs smiled peaceably and said that he appreciated the sergeant's reservations but his own duty was clear. The child was in trouble. His job was to bring succour to the troubled. He stepped into the street and walked forward.

The sergeant was faced with the dilemma of either leaving

Father Dobbs unsupported or of disobeying his own orders. He chose to disobey his orders. He unbuckled his equipment, gave it with his weapon to a corporal, and strode off, feeling naked, after Father Dobbs.

When the sergeant caught up with him, Father Dobbs was already crouched down, talking to the little girl. He had an arm around her shoulders, was cleaning her face with his handkerchief and was chatting soothingly to her. At first she continued to sniffle. Then she began to smile, then to giggle. Father Dobbs laughed too. So did the sergeant, by now squatting on his hunkers and, in between laughing, looking carefully around him.

A few people, men and women, drifted out from the doors of nearby houses. Their numbers grew. They formed a ring around the little group of the padre, the sergeant and the child. They seemed to be grimly hostile. They said nothing. The sergeant felt even more naked.

Father Dobbs, relaxed and serene, holding the girl by the hand, stood up slowly. He looked benevolently at the crowd. He addressed them, simply. He made no reference to recent events. He spoke only of friendship, and of love, and of the need for people to get on with their neighbours even when they disagreed with them, and of the goodness of God. His audience stayed silent, but there was a change in the quality of the silence. In an indescribable way, said the sergeant to the monsignor, the hatred began to evaporate. Father Dobbs was almost hypnotic when he spoke like that. The sergeant had seen it before, although never in a situation like this one. The padre's eyes fastened on those to whom he was not so much talking as confiding, and they were suddenly totally with him.

And then came the miracle. Most of the padre's *ad hoc* congregation were ordinary-looking working men, housewives, youths in jeans and teenage girls. But there were two who worried the sergeant. They were skinheads, with vacant, sullen expressions. They were dressed in studded denim jackets with the sleeves cut away, heavy steel-tipped boots and bicycle chains slung around their necks. There was elaborate tattooing upon their tightly muscled biceps and

154

forearms. The tattoos were indecipherable at a distance. The sergeant assumed them to be terse versions of Orange slogans. But one device, repeated, stood out. Each man, on each forearm, displayed a large swastika. They had one other thing in common. The faces of both were covered in acne.

The sergeant hoped that Father Dobbs would have the sense to ignore these two. Father Dobbs, with his instinct for picking out those most in need of help, did no such thing. He fixed his mesmeric gaze upon them, and invited them to come forward. Surprisingly, they did.

'We'll try a little experiment,' said Father Dobbs, cheerfully. 'I know, as you know although you won't admit it to anyone else, that what bothers you most in the world is the state of your faces. It's nothing to be ashamed of. It's a combination of your ages and bad luck. But it makes you aggressive, to want to hit out and hurt. Let's try to cure it, together. There are, you know, biblical precedents.'

The skinheads, and the spectators, stood quiet and still. The only word that the sergeant could think of when he was describing it to the monsignor was spellbound. The sergeant felt pretty spellbound himself.

It was a hot, dry day. Father Dobbs knelt and prayed. Then, still on his knees, he scooped up two handfuls of dust from the rubble in the street. He spat into them, repeatedly, and collected more dust, and spat again. He worked the mixture into a paste. He added some convenient dog dirt, and stirred that in too. When it was ready he examined it, and stood up. Slowly, he wiped the paste over the two faces, checking carefully that there were no gaps, putting the final touches with a last instalment of dust and spit. He instructed the patients to raise their faces towards the sun, and to stay unmoving until the paste was dry. During this interlude Father Dobbs knelt and prayed again. Not a word was said by either the skinheads or the crowd.

The monsignor, who had been taking notes, put down his pen at this point. He looked up.

'And they were cured?' he asked, softly.

'No,' said the sergeant. 'The stuff had no effect at all. the miracle was that they didn't fucking kill him.'

155

TINGE OF EMBARRASSMENT

THE initial suggestion, a modest one, came from the company commander of an infantry battalion in County Fermanagh. His company's tour, he said, had so far been fairly uneventful and he had been able to deal with almost everything that had come his way. There had been one exception that might develop into a category of exceptions.

A young cyclist, stopped at a roadblock and asked routinely to account for himself, had insisted upon replying in the Irish language. There was nothing whatsoever against the man, nothing suspicious about what he was carrying and nothing illegal about his talking in Irish. But his refusal to respond intelligibly to monoglot British troops made it necessary to detain him and to pass him on to the Royal Ulster Constabulary for further interrogation. Lawyers and politicians had then joined noisily in the act, which they may well have inspired in the first place, and there had followed rousing denunciations about the army's iniquity in violating fundamental civil rights by persecuting a patriot for the so-called offence of speaking his national tongue in his own country.

The publicity attendant upon this ploy had been so heady that imitators were beginning to take it up in increasing numbers. Candidates for painless martyrdom, accompanied by offended-looking witnesses mentally drafting news releases, were presenting themselves for examination and hoped-for arrest. The company commander had instructed his checkpoint NCOs to use their discretion in allowing unimpeded passage to patent tryers-on, but sooner or later a more damaging propaganda coup would inevitably be attempted. An Irish-speaking wanted Provo might, for example, brazen his way through a roadblock. His triumph would be celebrated in the Republican press with much wounding scorn and derision about the army's brutality being matched by its incapacity.

A useful counter would be to have a small pool of Irish-speaking soldiers available in the Province. These could be moved at random from checkpoint to checkpoint. Their presence would simultaneously discountenance the jokers, demonstrate that the army was not implacably hostile to the legitimate aspirations of the nationalist minority and probably generate some healthy entertainment. Local inquiries suggested that the standard of proficiency in the national language possessed by northern republicans was not high. To most, its acquisition was a painfully performed patriotic duty and its daily use minimal. A confrontation between one of these hesitant linguists and a fluent Irish speaker in British uniform would be, well, interesting.

The recommendation, supported at each stage, made its way through battalion headquarters, brigade headquarters, and the GOC Northern Ireland to the Ministry of Defence. There it was endorsed. The computer showed, as was expected, that the British army carried no Irish speakers on its strength. There was a reasonable number of soldiers with potential for language training. The project was put in the hands of a major in the Royal Army Educational Corps who was enjoined to select six suitable candidates, find an instructor through his academic contacts and run the course in conditions of secrecy. There was no real operational reason for secrecy. It was simply felt that if some nosey parker of a journalist got on to it too soon the army might be made to look rather silly and the planned surprises at Irish checkpoints would be blown in advance.

The RAEC major, an unworldly devotee of culture, took his instructions seriously. Since he didn't need to know he wasn't told the purpose of his activities. He assumed from his ungarnished orders that he was at the centre of some complex

Intelligence initiative, and he comported himself accordingly, over-influenced by John Le Carré and Ian Fleming. He was at first worried by the thought that any instructor in Irish must, almost by definition, be potentially hostile, and was relieved to find that the man suggested, a former school teacher from the Donegal Gaeltacht who lived with a married daughter in Norwich, had been a wartime officer in the Royal Naval Volunteer Reserve. Told mysteriously by the major, who wore a tweed suit and dark glasses, and who claimed unconvincingly to represent an unheard-of foundation for Celtic studies, to keep his mouth shut, the instructor contemplated the generous size of his fee and saw no reason to open it. The six candidates, spirited unexpectedly from the rigours of square bashing and saluting, told to dress in civilian clothes, to let their hair grow and furnished with a handsome lodging allowance while they studied a subject that they found absorbing, were cooperative about security too. They knew a good thing when they saw it.

The instructor was a good instructor. The students were well-chosen students. At the end of eight months of hard work the instructor held a protracted examination. He pronounced five of the six to be above average. The sixth was rated outstanding. He added a rider to his report. He pointed out that since he was both teacher and examiner, with a vested interest in certifying good results, it would be wise if there were to be an independent evaluation. The best place for this, he added, would be the Donegal Gaeltacht. He grinned to himself when he signed this recommendation. He had held to his bargain to keep his mouth shut, but he was no fool and he had service experience. The major's fragile pretences and the conscientious adoption of civilian habits by his pupils had not deceived him.

The major now found himself in a professional dilemma. He had done precisely what he had been told to do. He had not been told, he wrote, the purpose behind what he had been instructed to do. He had no intention of speculating. But all other things being equal, and he accepted that they probably weren't, he as an educationalist could only recommend that

158

his task would be incomplete unless the students were put to a practical test of their proficiency in an Irish-speaking area of Ireland. There was none in the north. His researches had shown that there were three major ones in the Irish Republic. There were significant variations between the usage in Kerry, Connemara and Donegal. The students had been taught the Donegal version. Therefore, to finish the job off thoroughly, the students should be given a field test in the Donegal Gaeltacht.

The major's submission was duly circulated within the Ministry of Defence for comment. The first commentator, supported strongly by the next three, said that the idea was politically preposterous. There was already enough trouble with the government of the Republic about patrols who strayed across a largely unmarked border, and about allegations that the SAS and RUC undercover teams repeatedly operated in the south, without adding gratuitously to the risk of diplomatic friction. The six linguists should be posted to Northern Ireland without further ado and let loose to try their luck for the purposes for which they had been trained. If they were no good, too bad. Not much would have been lost.

The fifth commentator, from the Intelligence staff, had other ideas. He was in a minority of one, but weight was given to his opinions because he was a thoughtful officer who always did his homework thoroughly, and who argued persuasively. He challenged the safe orthodoxies of his colleagues. Thanks to the initiative of a company commander serving in Northern Ireland, and to the endeavours of a major in the RAEC, there were six Irish-speaking soldiers on the strength. To ignore this asset would, in the Intelligence context, be folly.

The arguments so far put forward against sending soldiers in civilian clothes into the Republic on a woolly-minded errand to improve their language skills were soundly based and valid. But was not this open to exploitation?

Historically, the extreme forms of Irish nationalism had had links with traditional native Irish culture. It followed that there was a reasonable supposition that most of the inhabitants of the Donegal Gaeltacht favoured the establishment of a united Ireland, and that at a fair guess some at least gave moral, financial and logistic backing to the IRA and the INLA who were up to their lethal tricks just over the county boundary in County Derry. It would be useful to know more of this.

An opportunity now presented itself. Hundreds of thousands of British tourists visited Ireland every year. One extra young man among them would not be noticed. If he happened to speak fluent Irish, and if he happened to make his way to Donegal, he might pick up all sorts of interesting information simply by hanging around the pubs and keeping his eyes and ears open. The RAEC major's passion for secrecy fortuitously provided an excellent cover story should anything go wrong.

The selected soldier could be briefed simply to go ahead and perfect his Irish. He would be advised that for obvious reasons of personal safety he should not disclose his profession, and he would be asked in passing to report back anything of possible security interest that he picked up. All briefing would be through the major, who would be told that it was primarily an educational venture. The soldier would not suspect, because he would neither see nor be seen by any Intelligence officer that he was being employed on a low-key Intelligence enterprise. If he were unlucky enough to be questioned he could only answer, with complete truth, that he was an advanced language student.

The minority recommendation prevailed. The RAEC major was told to get a more explicit certificate from the instructor about the best of his pupils. The instructor gladly certified that Mr Ron Harris was a highly gifted man, who for practical purposes was bilingual in Irish and English.

A scrutiny of Corporal Harris's service records was supplemented by discreet inquiries of the officers under whom he had served. All sources were encouraging. Harris was a conspicuously intelligent young NCO with a firm grasp of his duties, a determined personality, a preoccupation with physical fitness and an ambition to get on in the army. He neither smoked nor drank and looked upon drugs with abhorrence. He had been earmarked for accelerated promotion to sergeant. Harris could almost have been designed for the job.

On a sunny July morning Harris, in jeans, windcheater and with a rucksack, caught the Holyhead train from Euston station. He felt pleased with himself, and pleased with his choice of soldiering as a career. It had never occurred to him when he joined that he would be sent on a month's holiday at public expense, instructed to travel to wherever he thought best to refine his knowledge of a language that he found enchanting. An elliptically worded injunction to be on the lookout for anything that might be of counter-insurgency significance, and a more robust piece of advice not to disclose that he was a British soldier, added a taste of excitement and adventure to what promised to be an enjoyable jaunt. Throughout the train journey and the boat crossing to Dun Laoghaire he sat in silent contentment, lost in his grammar and his dictionary.

From Busarus in Dublin he caught a coach to Donegal. He was disappointed to find that his fellow-passengers spoke exclusively in English, but once he arrived and travelled about, and got to know people, he felt entirely at home. The Norwich instructor had earned his pay. Harris's mastery of pronunciation, syntax and colloquialisms was almost indistinguishable from those of a people whose ancestors had spoken their ancient tongue from before Christ's arrival on earth.

In the Department of External Affairs in Dublin it was decided to deal with the problem with an absence of official fuss. The graph of the temperature of Anglo–Irish relations, which for the past fifteen years had moved shakily along a progression of troughs and peaks, was rising towards one of the peaks. The Taoiseach was being briefed for one of his *à deux* discussions with the British Prime Minister when the two met at the EEC summit in Brussels. Irritants that might cloud the pure air of the talk must be eliminated with calculated casualness. This one was a clear case for an off-the-record hint. A diplomatic cocktail party was the obvious vehicle. The

British defence attaché seemed to be the best recipient of the signal.

He was swilling the Jameson around the bottom of his glass, smiling fixedly at a harangue from a deranged feminist sculptress and wondering how soon he could decently get the hell out. A familiar, friendly face appeared beside him.

'Hallo, Derek,' said the face.

'Hallo, Michael. How are you?' said the defence attaché with relief. 'Do you know . . .?'

'Delia and I have known each other for years.'

'Too many years,' said Delia. 'I'm off.' She went.

'Can I have a quiet word?' said Michael. They moved to a lonely corner, where potplants had been misused as ashtrays by some of the cruder guests.

'The word is,' said Michael, 'that the sooner you get your man out of Donegal, the better. Otherwise we'll have to put him out. Then there'll be a public row.'

The defence attaché looked at him carefully.

'To the best of my knowledge,' he said, 'we haven't got a man in Donegal.'

'To the best of mine, you have. He's an Irish speaker. Not just any old Irish speaker. He's brilliant. I'm told that his Irish is indistinguishable from that of native speakers. He sounds as if he's lived there all his life.'

The defence attaché considered this.

'Michael,' he said, after a long pause, 'I'll have it looked into. Without prejudice to my denial, or whatever the appropriate diplomatic bullshit is. But may I ask you a question? If this fellow who you say we have there, and I say we haven't, is indistinguishable from a native Irish speaker, how do you know that he's not a native Irish speaker? Are you sure there isn't some mistake? As I understand it, there's always been a great deal of emigration from Donegal. Could your people not have picked on some harmless poor chap who's been away for years, possibly since he was a child, and who . . .'

'No,' said Michael, 'our people couldn't. He's black.'

162

ONE ROUND UP THE SPOUT

AMONG the more unpromising recruits to report to the Fusiliers' depot in 1938 was Arthur Hogg, a stooped youth with pimples and several grievances. He was from a broken home. He had been consistently unemployed since he had left school at the age of fourteen. He had been in minor trouble with the police ('victimization').

He did not keep these sorrows to himself. He doggedly accumulated others and whined endlessly about them all. He had joined the army, he said repetitively, because it offered free food, clothing and housing. He found all three to be inferior. He disliked the work and the manner in which he had to earn them.

He progressed complainingly and reluctantly to a platoon in the 2nd Battalion. His pimples had moderated and his stoop had been unstooped on the square. He had put on about half a stone in weight. These physical developments were unmatched by any change of outlook.

'That new lad Hogg wants watching, sir,' said his platoon sergeant after a week.

Hogg's platoon commander, a subaltern wise beyond his years, watched Hogg. His conclusions were different from the sergeant's. Hogg, he thought, had potential. Get behind the protective cloud of self-pity, apply a nicely adjusted mixture of coercion and encouragement and something might be made of Hogg.

The sergeant attended to the coercion. Hogg, having discovered to his dissatisfaction and by unhappy trial and error that he wouldn't be able to get away with substandard turnout, sullen discourtesy and protracted feigned inability to strip and reassemble the Lewis gun, gave up trying. He conformed resentfully but did the minimum required of him.

The encouragement leg of Hogg's reclamation was based upon the observation that he was athletic and intelligent, both qualities hitherto unexploited. The subaltern's starting point was the athleticism. He had noticed Hogg's stamina, displayed with an accompanying expression of bitterness, on long route marches. An almost mutinous Hogg was put into training for cross-country running. The subaltern trained with him and coached him. Hogg, finding himself for the first time in his life doing something that he was naturally good at, began to enjoy it. He enjoyed it even more when, entered for the Northern Command championships, he came in second and won a small silver-plated cup. Winning a prize, like doing a difficult thing well, was a new experience for him.

On the day after the race the subaltern, who had come in first, had a long, friendly private talk with Hogg. Many years later Hogg, looking back on his career, was to identify two of its principal strands as dating from this conversation. The first was the small beginnings of a realization that if he modified some of his prejudices he might actually start to like soldiering and to become good at it. The second was the birth of a respect and affection, subsequently growing to hero-worship, for the man who was later to be General Sir James Harrison.

A summary of Hogg's next thirty years reads like one of those improving Victorian stories for boys, replete with manly endeavour, pluck, stirring adventure and virtue's reward.

Fusilier Hogg, further coached by Harrison, was selected to play soccer and hockey for his battalion. He reached the semi-finals of the welterweight division of the army boxing championships at the Albert Hall.

Fusilier Hogg, still in Harrison's platoon, went to France with the British Expeditionary Force in 1939, and came out again rather more precipitately through Dunkirk in 1940.

Sergeant Hogg, of Major Harrison's company, was awarded the Military Medal in Tunisia in 1943, after a deed of what the citation described as of outstanding gallantry,

*'Fall out the man who wrote a letter to 'My Scrumptious Bit of Sugar' and signed himself 'Your
Great Big Curly-headed Boy,' and report at once to the Battalion Censor.'*

resourcefulness and leadership on Long Stop Hill.

Company Sergeant Major Hogg, shot in both legs at
Cassino while trying to bring in a man wounded by close-
range Spandau fire, was in turn brought back by a party led in
person by Lieutenant Colonel Harrison, who as usual was well
up with the forward troops and was indifferent to criticisms
that commanding officers should leave that kind of thing to
subordinates whose military educations had cost less than his
had.

At the Gothic Line, Regimental Sergeant Major Hogg
demonstrated his belief that one good turn deserved another
by dumping the replenishment ammunition that he was
delivering exactly where it should have been dumped, and by
formally asking permission of the second in command to go in
search of the colonel, who had been reported by wireless as
badly hit while visiting a company that was being counter-
attacked. The second in command assented because, as he
explained later, 'the RSM would have bloody well gone
whether I said he could or not.'

RSM Hogg, under heavy fire, reached the company posi-

165

tion, found that all the officers were casualties, took over, organized the repulse of the counterattack, awaited the arrival of a replacement for the company commander and, still being comprehensively shot at, supervised the extrication of all the wounded, including Colonel Harrison.

Lieutenant Hogg, commissioned in the field, saw the rest of the war out in Italy. Afterwards, as a quartermaster, he served in Palestine, Malaya, Aden and Cyprus. Brigadier Harrison was soon moving on to higher things elsewhere, but the two kept in touch by the exchange of Christmas cards and by the passing of messages of goodwill through mutual friends. They met when, infrequently, they were in the same country at the same time.

Hogg preserved throughout an abiding gratitude and admiration for Harrison. Hogg could see no prospect of his ever being able to repay what he saw as an incalculable debt for the transformation of his life. The opportunity for repayment came when Harrison's son Robert was commissioned into the regiment in 1968.

The battalion was at Aldershot at the time. Captain and Quartermaster Hogg had a year to go before retirement, to which he was not looking forward. He was the oldest soldier in the unit, a decorated legend greatly venerated and rather feared.

Those few who knew him well detected a soft streak tempered by a strange romanticism beneath a grimly austere surface. In a cynical era Hogg held to old-fashioned beliefs, perhaps myths. One of Harrison's earlier services to Hogg had been his encouraging Hogg to read. Hogg had responded cautiously to the advice, but in a limited way had profited from it. He had soon established a literary boundary beyond which he had no interest in proceeding. Hogg read and reread military fiction, Kipling, P. C. Wren and A. E. W. Mason. Those of Hogg's values not absorbed from Harrison came direct from *Soldiers Three*, *Beau Geste* and *The Four Feathers*. Hogg in the 1960s held to a code of conduct that Kipling *et al* had celebrated, not always convincingly, as being common military currency a generation or two previously. Hogg, so far as he could and sometimes with unnerving results, applied these precepts to his role in the modern army.

He had confidently expected to find in young Robert Harrison all the qualities, inherited and Kiplingesque, that he most admired. Second Lieutenant R. Harrison lacked almost every one of them. Within a week of his joining the battalion he had made himself universally disliked, and had inspired the doctor to reflective thought about regressive genes.

Young Harrison was surly, self-opiniated and complaining. In appearance he was slovenly. He did as little work as he could, and he did it badly. He was overbearing and sarcastic in his dealings with the soldiers. They detested him. He did not try to hide the contemptuous resentment that he seemed to feel for his brother officers, and he made it worse by whingeing to anyone who would listen (very few) about the personal injustices to which he claimed that he was subjected by his company commander, by the adjutant and by his colonel. He was, in short, a disaster. Had he not been the son of a distinguished father who had served the regiment brilliantly, Second Lieutenant Harrison would have been thrown out within his first three months.

Hogg was appalled. He became more so as he slowly realized that he had come across all the more unlovely of young Harrison's characteristics once before, in his own early life. Harrison was not the expected replica of his father. Allowing for differences of family background and education, Harrison was a walking image of that deplorable recruit Fusilier Hogg of thirty years before, rescued from ignominious uselessness by the intervention of Harrison's father.

This, painful though it was, was Hogg's chance to repay his debt to Harrison senior, now Deputy Chief of the Defence Staff.

Hogg pondered, with concentration.

He asked himself the question that he always asked himself when faced with a troublesome conundrum. What would Harrison senior have done in the circumstances? In this case the answer was obvious. Harrison senior, long ago, had dealt with an almost identical problem posed by the young Fusilier Hogg. The old Captain Hogg couldn't involve himself with the young Second Lieutenant in all that physical stuff about coercion and the development of nascent pride in athleticism, but he could certainly talk to Harrison in the way in which Harrison's father had once talked to him. He invited Harrison to his room in the mess for a private chat.

It was a fiasco. Robert Harrison listened impatiently to a contrived, avuncular piece of frank advice about his performance to date and his prospects for the future. Robert commented upon this. He at first alternated argumentative-ness with surliness, and then he became offensive. He hated the army, he said. He'd been brought up in the bloody army. He'd had the army dinned into him for as long as he could remember. He'd gone to Sandhurst and was where he was now simply because without consultation it had been assumed by his father that that was what he would do. And as no one knew better than Hogg, nobody stood up to Robert's father.

Since this was a private talk with no witnesses, Robert said, there was a bit more that he had to say. Who the hell did a jumped-up ranker like Hogg think he was, preaching like a bloody scoutmaster? If Hogg had chosen to spend his life as a registered arse-licker, saying Yes sir, No sir, Three bags full sir, to Robert's father, that was Hogg's affair, but it gave him no right to . . .

Hogg, his face darkened by fury, knotted tendons in his neck obtruding, told Robert Harrison to get out. Robert went, sneering.

Hogg, superficially relaxed, professionally as coolly efficient as ever, passed the next few weeks in a personal agony of angry indecision. His commonsense told him that his reaction to Robert Harrison's boorish incivilities had been natural and right. Two other jangling components of his thoughts reminded him insistently that he had failed. By losing his temper, rightly, with young Harrison, he had sacrificed his only possible chance of doing something constructive to repay his debt to Harrison's father. In the meeting of that responsibility he had been selfishly inadequate.

Upon this piece of remorse was superimposed another, darker, conflicting consideration. Robert Harrison had insulted him. And he had done so in terms that were so unambiguous that Hogg, notably when he had had a drink or two, and when he had related the insult to what the response of Beau Geste or of one of Kipling's heroes would have been, left him feeling even more of a failure. Going back a bit beyond Kipling, reflected Hogg when this aspect of the matter was foremost in his mind, he would have issued a challenge to a duel and to hell with Harrison's father, who would in any case have put honour above consanguinity and would have approved, aloofly.

This sort of thinking, shapeless and undisciplined, got Hogg nowhere. In calmer moments he recognized its ineffectiveness. The only course open to him, he calculated, was the unsatisfactory one of waiting and seeing and reacting to developments.

In the meantime he spoke to Robert Harrison only when it was essential to do so in the course of duty. Harrison continued to move self-destructively from one sullen imbroglio to the next.

The matter of the discrepancy in the mess funds came to light from a random audit. The officer who normally acted as the mess treasurer was away on a course. Young Harrison, partly as a measure to broaden his experience, partly from a spirit of punitive retribution, had been ordered to deputize for him. Hogg was responsible for checking the accounts at any times convenient to him within set periods of three months. On this occasion he chose to do the job on a Saturday afternoon when everybody else was away.

Over £40 in cash was missing. Harrison had initialled acceptance of the cash float from the mess sergeant on the previous day. Hogg looked miserably at the account book. At breakfast he had overheard Harrison talking of his day's plans. He had said that he was going racing at Goodwood. No detective work was necessary.

Hogg thought for a while and then went for a long walk. He thought further during the walk. When he came back he showered, changed and returned to the ante-room, where he started drinking. After a lonely dinner he dismissed the mess waiter and resumed drinking. Later still, he told the barman to stand down. No point in his wasting his evening to serve one officer, said Hogg. Leave out the bottle and he'd serve himself. He'd put the chits for collection in the morning.

Hogg continued with his thinking and drinking. At a late point in the combined process he reached a decision. It wasn't a particularly good one, but it was the best that he could come up with. It was in two parts. The first committed Hogg to a compromise with his conscience. The second, drastic and final, was of the stuff that to a younger generation, Robert Harrison prominent among them, was fit only for satirical television shows. There was nothing amusing about it to Hogg's mind. He was in deadly earnest.

He went to his room and collected the Luger that he had taken from a captured German officer in Italy. Hogg checked the action and loaded the magazine. He brought the gun back to the ante-room and poured himself another drink. He was beginning to feel a little muddled.

He toyed absently with the pistol, rehearsing while he did so the precise wording of the two-part ultimatum that he would deliver to Robert Harrison when he returned to barracks on the Sunday evening. Hogg was still going through his lines, the pistol serving as an aide-mémoire, when he heard the sound of a car drawing up outside the mess. The engine was revved up and then switched off. Footsteps approached. Robert Harrison came into the ante-room.

He was, as usual, feeling sorry for himself. Also as usual, he lacked all inhibition about confiding the reason for his sorrow to the nearest live human. The fact that he and Hogg had not exchanged an unofficial word since that abrasive discussion in Hogg's room seemed not to trouble him at all.

'Bloody horses,' said Harrison, helping himself from the bottle that had been left out. 'Every one a bloody loser.'

Hogg cleared his throat.

'I want to speak to you,' he said dangerously.

Harrison ignored him.

'Couldn't even afford to take my bird out to dinner,' said

Harrison. 'Had to run her home. End of *that* bit of lovelife.'

'I want to speak to you,' said Hogg again.

Harrison looked at him, as if recognizing him for the first time.

'What about?' said Harrison. He sounded irritated, distracted from what *he* had to say.

'I'll tell you what about,' said Hogg, levelly. 'About forty pounds and a little bit more missing from the mess funds.'

Harrison tried to bluster it out. He wasn't very successful. His hand shook, and he spilled some of his drink.

'Oh, that,' he said.

'Yes. That. You needn't waste time in buggering about. It could only have been you.'

'Yes,' said Harrison, after a pause. He was working himself up to defiance.

Hogg gave him little chance to develop it.

'What I was going to do,' said Hogg, fiddling about with the Luger, 'was to break the good habits of a lifetime. Not for your miserable sake. For your father's sake. I was going to say, Look, only you and I know about this. Only you or I could have pinched that forty quid. So if you'd just quietly paid it back out of your winnings I'd have let you do that after giving you a bollocking that you wouldn't have forgotten. But it won't work, will it? You haven't got any bloody winnings. Have you?'

'No,' said Harrison. He hadn't achieved satisfactory defiance. He was paler now.

'So we come to part two of what I was going to say,' said Hogg reasonably. 'You won't like it as much as you would have liked part one.'

Harrison stared at him. Hogg was very calm and very sinister. He spoke easily, quietly.

'Part two,' said Hogg, 'involves something that you know nothing about. Your father does. I do. But you don't. It's called honour. Makes you snigger probably. It doesn't make me even smile. I take it seriously. I'm going to give you a chance to redeem yours.'

Harrison continued to stare at him. Hogg drank a large gulp

from his glass.

'You have only two options really,' said Hogg conversation- ally. 'The first is to face a charge of embezzlement. You'd be court-martialled and cashiered. You'd be chucked out of the army in disgrace. You'd probably never get a proper job again. None of which would bother me in the least. It's all you bloody deserve. What *does* bother me is the effect that all that would have on your father. It would break him. So that brings us to the second option.'

He sank another huge slug of his drink. Harrison was begin- ning to look genuinely frightened.

'You'll doubtless try to dismiss the second option as absurdly old-fashioned and ridiculously melodramatic,' said Hogg. He slurred slightly the pronunciation of 'ridiculously'. 'Well, try as much as you like. Only don't bore me with it. Have a private little session of private little derision and then get down to facing some facts. There'll be nobody else in the mess until early tomorrow morning. You've got the whole night to choose from. Just take this, go away to your room and do it.' He reversed the Luger in his hand, and held it out, butt first.

Harrison, shaking like a malaria sufferer, tried to speak. He could get no words out. He made rumbling noises in his throat. At last he achieved a croak.

'You're mad,' he said. He made no move to accept the pistol.

'Not in the least,' said Hogg equably. 'Entirely rational. I've been around long enough to know that there are no really neat solutions. This is the neatest that I can think of.'

He became suddenly, incisively impatient, the issuer of an order who had long been accustomed to instant obedience.

'Take it,' he snapped. The wrist of the hand that held the muzzle of the pistol jerked rhythmically. The butt waggled, like a metronome set to fast.

Harrison stretched out a shaking hand. He grasped the butt, turned the gun around, held it close to his face and stared down the barrel. He stayed silent and unmoving, eyes dilated, for some seconds. Hogg watched him closely. He saw Harrison swallow twice, with difficulty. Harrison's mouth began to move. His two words were whispered, almost inaudible. 'All right,' said Harrison.

Hogg was surprised at the speed with which Harrison translated decision into action. The crash of the pistol's discharge, magnified by the enclosing walls and ceiling of the ante-room, followed the All right within two seconds.

Everything that had to be done was, naturally, done in a seemly manner. The death of an officer by a self-inflicted pistol wound inflicted in his own mess could not of course be hushed up, but some benevolent perjury and a tolerant court of inquiry ensured that the tragedy would be recorded as an accident. The money was repaid discreetly. The scandal of its abstraction never became known outside the battalion. There was a military funeral with full honours, a firing party, a bugler to play the sad, sweet notes of the Last Post. General Harrison, grimly impassive, saluted the grave and went quietly away.

That same evening he poured himself a drink and sat reflectively beside the fire in his sitting room. He spoke at length of what had happened and of what had led up to it. He was never to mention the matter again. The conclusion that he had reached, he said, had nothing new about it, but familiarity made it no less painful. However close you were to someone, however well you thought that you knew them, there was always some unsuspected part of them that remained hidden, secret. Every living man had a concealed weakness in his make-up.

The general's son Robert agreed. Hogg must have been a great fellow in the heady days of wartime soldiering, said Robert, but it hadn't taken Robert long to realize that Hogg was systematically pilfering from the mess funds.